Further acclaim for
Rubies in the Orchard

★(Starred Review)
"In a forest of dry marketing books, [Lynda] Resnick's animated debut stands out as its own hidden gem, filled with juicy real-life tales of marketing . . . The author charms with her winning wit and a self-deprecating tone as she distills the secrets of her extraordinary career . . . A must-read for anyone who aspires to Resnick's level of promotional genius, success, or commitment to environmental sustainability."

—*Publishers Weekly*

"Lynda Resnick is one of the great marketers of our time—who else, after all, could have rebranded and relaunched a food as troublesome as the pomegranate, a fruit formerly more trouble to eat than it was worth? Whether you're in the business of selling products or ideas, *Rubies in the Orchard* is full of indispensable advice. Even better, it manages to delight even as it instructs."

—MICHAEL POLLAN, author of
The Omnivore's Dilemma and *In Defense of Food*

"There are pearls of wisdom in *Rubies in the Orchard*—wisdom that marketing genius Lynda Resnick has gained through long experience, hard work, and dealing with many challenges on the road to her outstanding success. In sharing her personal life story she gives us very useful tips about discovering real value in the world around us and making best use of it. An inspiring book and a good read!"

—DR. ANDREW WEIL, MD, author of
Healthy Aging and *8 Weeks to Optimum Health*

"An inspiring story and an enthralling treatise by one of America's most imaginative and energetic entrepreneurs . . . Lynda Resnick, the POM Queen, shows each of us that it's possible to do well by doing good."
—ROBERT F. KENNEDY JR., award-winning author
and president of Waterkeeper Alliance

"Lynda Resnick understands popular culture, she reads it brilliantly and places her products in a context that uses popular energy to advance them."
—DAVID GEFFEN, founder, Asylum and Geffen Records;
co-founder, DreamWorks SKG

"Part marketing master class, part can't-put-it-down biography, *Rubies in the Orchard* is as refreshing as a cold bottle of FIJI Water on a hot day and as fortifying as a glass of POM juice. Read this witty and wise book to learn how to sell your brand . . . but, whatever you do, read it. It sparkles as brightly as the gem in its title."
—ARIANNA HUFFINGTON, editor in chief, The Huffington Post

"Exactly the spirit we need to deal with the gloom and doom of Wall Street. I read it cover to cover without stopping. I felt emboldened."
—FRANK GEHRY, architect

"*Rubies in the Orchard* is the can't-put-it-down, remember-every-word, must-read book of our era! Read it, enjoy it . . . and tell your friends everywhere to do the same!"
—KEVIN KLOSE, president, NPR

"Irving Berlin said of Fred Astaire that he was 'the purest talent' with whom he had ever worked. As to marketing and original creation, Lynda Resnick is the purest talent and her writing, irresistible."
—DAVID G. BRADLEY, chairman, Atlantic Media Group

"Lynda Resnick is one of America's great brand builders. *Rubies in the Orchard* is a strategic marketing primer wrapped in a witty narrative that celebrates the seller's honesty and the consumer's sense of value."
—MICHAEL MILKEN, chairman, Milken Institute

"If pomegranates are the rubies in the orchard, then this book is the diamond on the bookshelf. This book sparkles with Lynda Resnick's expertise in marketing and is flawless, a perfect gem on how to see the best in what is sometimes a rough stone."

—RITA WILSON, actor, producer

"*Rubies in the Orchard* talks about real experiences with products that are good for people, marketed in a conscientious way. Real-life stuff, involving balancing business and social concerns."

—CRAIG NEWMARK, founder and CEO, Craigslist

"Lynda Resnick has done Adam Smith one better: she has given the business world a much-needed face-lift and a sense of humor. *Rubies in the Orchard* is a twenty-first-century *Wealth of Nations* for every man and every woman who has ever dreamed of starting a business and marketing it effectively. Above all else, it is a charming memoir of one of the truly brilliant entrepreneurs of our time."

—DR. HENRY LOUIS GATES, JR.,
Alphonse Fletcher University Professor, Harvard University

"Lynda Resnick is a genius at marketing. In this wonderful new book, she reveals her potent secret: meeting the most powerful yet unmet human needs for integrity, quality, and sustainability as well as for love and community . . . *Rubies in the Orchard* is the new bible of marketing."

—DR. DEAN ORNISH, founder and president,
Preventive Medicine Research Institute

"A 'must-read' for anyone interested in selling or marketing. Lynda Resnick is a master marketer, and we can all learn from her."

—LEONARD LAUDER, chairman of the board,
The Estée Lauder Companies

"A candid and sharp analysis of today's world of product marketing. Lynda Resnick has generously offered the truth behind her success, which is a refreshing combination of authenticity, value, and transparency in marketing."

—ALICE WATERS, bestselling author,
founder, and co-owner, Chez Panisse

"Everybody playing and toiling and wanting to achieve success with a brand in our difficult economy should read this book to understand right from wrong, good from bad, quality from junk."
—MICHAEL EISNER, founder, Tornante Company, and former chairman and CEO, The Walt Disney Company

"Lynda Resnick humbly resists being called a marketing genius. Read her book at the risk of becoming one yourself."
—NORMAN LEAR , award-winning television and film writer, director, and producer

"This illuminating, captivating, and sassy book has it all—marketing savvy, life values, and a clear path to success no matter what your goal."
—BARBARA GOLDSMITH, bestselling author and historian

"Lynda Resnick is one dynamic, persuasive gal. She can talk anybody into anything, including getting me to write a blurb for this book. Now that's persuasive."
—LARRY DAVID, star of HBO's *Curb Your Enthusiasm*

"Lynda Resnick is a force of nature and a force for good. She is also a brilliant marketer. *Rubies in the Orchard* reveals the secret of her success—effective marketing is not about fooling people but respecting them."
—MICHAEL SANDEL, professor of government, Harvard University, and author of *Public Philosophy: Essays on Morality in Politics*

"With insight, elegance, and simplicity [Lynda Resnick] has become an icon in the world of marketing. We should be so lucky that a little of her magic might rub off on us all!"
—STEPHEN McPHERSON, president of ABC Entertainment

"Lynda Resnick is to branding what Warren Buffett is to investing: a master of honesty, common sense, and belief that one can do well while doing good."
—GLORIA STEINEM, bestselling author, feminist activist, and co-founder, *Ms.* and *New York* magazines

"A fascinating and instructive guide into the world of a marketing genius, told with a beguiling frankness and good humor."
—MICHAEL YORK, actor and author

"The single best piece of writing I have read in years by an active and successful CEO. Stop everything you're doing right now and take a swig of this honest and useful book."
—WARREN BENNIS, Distinguished Professor of Business Administration, University of Southern California, and author of *On Becoming a Leader*

"I recommend *Rubies in the Orchard* to marketers, business executives eager to unlearn bad lessons from business school, or anyone who has ever been sure they had a great idea but didn't have the confidence to get started."
—SETH SIEGEL co-founder and CEO, The Beanstalk Group

"Lynda Resnick is by far the absolute epicenter of future marketing where vision and language, form and appeal, attitude and personality, intelligence and spirit are all built into the product as to allow the Brand to speak and interact with the consumer . . . WOW!"
—PETER ARNELL, founder and CEO, The Arnell Group

"No one I know has more intuitive sense of consumer tastes and insight into what delights audiences more than Lynda Resnick. This wonderful book will be a catalyst to unlock the reader's strengths, skills, and abilities."
—BOBBY KOTICK, CEO, Activision

"From one Queen to another . . . Lynda Resnick, the POM Queen, has given us a crown jewel. *Rubies in the Orchard* is richly filled with insight from one of the cutting-edge marketers and entrepreneurs of our time."
—HER MAJESTY QUEEN NOOR OF JORDAN

"A captivating . . . read about visionary leadership and innovative marketing at its best."
—YORAM (JERRY) WIND, The Lauder Professor and professor of marketing, The Wharton School

"If there were one book that's a must-read for anyone trying to persuade people of the value of a product or to communicate to a mass audience why they should try something new, it is Lynda Resnick's fascinating, elegant, and succinct *Rubies in the Orchard*. Her wit, originality, and courage are infectious."

—LEON BOTSTEIN, president, Bard College, and music director and principal conductor, American Symphony Orchestra and Jerusalem Symphony Orchestra

"Lynda Resnick is smart, creative, and a doer. *Rubies in the Orchard* tells us how she thinks and how she makes great things happen in business . . . It's a good read authored by a good person."

—THE HONORABLE JON CORZINE, governor of New Jersey

"Highly entertaining and smartly funny . . . The marketing philosophy [Lynda Resnick] espouses in her book is so pure, powerful, deceptively simple, and easily adapted to any situation that it earns the ultimate marketing accolade . . . why didn't I think of that? *Rubies in the Orchard* should be required reading at every business school in the country."

—LEONARD GOLDBERG,
television and motion picture executive and producer

"The Resnicks have a true talent for building successful brands by combining product with great marketing. Lynda's superb creative marketing skills and respect for the integrity of the brand and the consumer is the critical element to establishing brands and creating great value. *Rubies in the Orchard* offers a revealing insight into the process and is a road map for creating profit while being socially responsible."

—TERRY SEMEL, chairman, Windsor Media,
and former chairman and CEO, Yahoo!

"Lynda [Resnick] proves that there is only so much you can learn in business school. The real world is where real learning happens. In *Rubies in the Orchard*, Lynda shows that it is not only great to produce the right results; it is also increasingly valuable to produce the right results the right way. Doing good is good for business. This is especially important in this demanding, informed, skeptical marketing world. Read it. Learn from it. And live it."

—LARRY LIGHT, chairman and CEO, Arcature LLC

"Lynda Resnick . . . weaves her magic through unmatched advertising campaigns, ingenious packaging, inspired product placements, inventive uses of the Internet, and surprising product extensions . . . a great story about a bold original, who inspires us to think differently."

—JUDY OLIAN, dean, UCLA Anderson School of Management

RUBIES
in the
ORCHARD

LYNDA RESNICK

with Francis Wilkinson

RUBIES
in the
ORCHARD

How to Uncover the

HIDDEN GEMS

in Your Business

DOUBLEDAY

New York ▪ *London* ▪ *Toronto* ▪ *Sydney* ▪ *Auckland*

DOUBLEDAY

Copyright © 2009 by Lynda Rae Resnick

All Rights Reserved

Published in the United States by Doubleday,
an imprint of The Doubleday Publishing Group,
a division of Random House, Inc., New York.
www.doubleday.com

DOUBLEDAY is a registered trademark and the DD colophon is
a trademark of Random House, Inc.

All trademarks are the property of their respective companies.

Book design by Judith Stagnitto Abbate / Abbate Design

The illustration credits on pages 193–94 are an extension
of this copyright page.

Library of Congress Cataloging-in-Publication Data
Resnick, Lynda.
Rubies in the orchard : how to uncover the hidden gems in
your business / by Lynda Resnick with Francis Wilkinson.
—1st ed.
p. cm.
"The POM Queen's secrets to building brands and marketing
just about anything." Includes index.
(hc : alk. paper)
1. Marketing. 2. Advertising. 3. Value. 4. Business.
I. Wilkinson, Francis. II. Title.
HF5415.R462 2009
658.8—dc22
2008023167

ISBN 978-0-385-52578-7

PRINTED IN THE UNITED STATES OF AMERICA

1   3   5   7   9   10   8   6   4   2

First Edition

For Stewart

CONTENTS

PREFACE

I t was the kind of March day we sometimes get in Los Angeles: crystal blue skies, a few wispy white clouds, 72 and sunny. To celebrate her birthday, my friend Laurie David had invited a few friends to join her on a hike in the Santa Monica Mountains.

With so many business responsibilities to attend to, I don't get to spend as much girl time as I would like; my female relationships are usually relegated to the phone or double dates with their men and mine. But this day was different. I had set aside time to celebrate, and there was nothing pulling me back to the office.

We sat around an old picnic table, drank pink champagne through straws, and consumed a scrumptious lunch of soft cheeses and hard salami, French bread and olives. It was a magical day, one that would change my life.

The friends around the table were a stunningly accomplished bunch. Laurie David was one of the first activists I met in the green movement. In addition to helping open my eyes to environmental issues, she had just produced Al Gore's powerful documentary, *An Inconvenient Truth.* Never one to let the green grass grow under her feet, Laurie was now busy writing a book for children on the subject.

Rita Wilson was just about to appear as Roxie in the Broadway show *Chicago.* A brilliant actress, she was preparing to show the world that she could sing and dance, as well. She was nervous and excited, fulfilling a dream she had silently coveted for years.

Arianna Huffington's blog was growing by leaps, and she seemed to be everywhere at once, speaking out about domestic and foreign policy, our dependence on Middle East oil, and countless other topics, all while writing her eleventh book and raising two wonderful girls.

When it was my turn to discuss my plans, however, the conversation grew suddenly quiet. It seemed I didn't have any plans. Yes, I enjoyed my business. My family was doing well and my husband and I were happy together. But my dreams seemed to have stagnated. I had accomplished many goals; now I struggled to think up a new one.

"What's your dream, Lynda?" they all asked. "What do you want to do that you have never done?"

Suddenly, I blurted out, "I want to write a book."

"Well, why don't you?"

At that moment, I made a commitment to them—and to myself—that I would.

"Write what you know" is wise advice for authors. What I know best is marketing and branding. I have had a long and successful career. And over the years, I have educated myself with a bit of help from some very smart friends, mentors, and employees. I've worked hard and benefited from my share of luck. But through trial and error, I've also developed a formula for success. That day in the Santa Monica hills, I realized I could share with others what has taken me four decades to learn on my own.

Business in the twenty-first century is different from what it was when I started all those years ago. It gets tougher every day. Markets are unpredictable, the economy is unstable, the environment is a challenge, and the uncertainties of globalization and terrorism and energy supply don't make things any easier. But forty years of facing—and more often than not overcoming—market challenges have given me a useful perspective on business along with specific insights into a range of marketing issues. I have a system now. And if it's a marketing or branding challenge, chances are I've confronted it somewhere along the line and figured out how to prevail—or at least how to survive.

Experience is an invaluable asset, one gained through a life lived with passion, commitment, and energy. Your business career will be different from mine. But I hope this book helps you develop your own formula for success. At the very least, you can see not only how I approach marketing and branding, but why. Success isn't a matter of throwing something against the wall in the hope that it will stick. It's the sum of research, focus, discipline, and hard work. It flows from a systematic approach to uncovering value that others have overlooked (perhaps because they were busy throwing stuff against a wall to see what would stick) and learning how to communicate that value in clever, effective, truthful ways.

It's sometimes hard in the chaos of the moment to stay focused on what truly works. I hope that in following the trail of my experiences, and the methods (and occasional madness) I have laid out in this book, you'll see a road map for your own success. Take a hike with me. Follow your dreams.

CHAPTER 1

An 8,000-Year-Old
Overnight Sensation

I had hit a personal low. I was out of work for the first time since I was seventeen. I had no job, a blank date book, and so much time on my hands I could lunch with the girls. Sure, I had money. But I was also a bit lost. The kids were grown and living their own lives. Without work, which had been central to my identity and my self-esteem for so many years, I was no longer sure who I was. I had been retired for two months, and already I was panicked.

My husband, Stewart, who was still very much in the thick of business and suffering none of my existential woes, invited me to attend a business meeting. He wanted me to serve as a sounding board for a new venture we had been working on for years. Maybe I would have something useful to say? Maybe. Maybe not.

Here was the situation: after having acquired more

than 100 acres of mature pomegranate trees in the San Joaquin Valley of California in 1987, Stewart had steadily planted hundreds of acres more throughout the 1990s. Like most crops, pomegranates were basically a commodity, albeit on a much smaller scale. But when the orchards were well managed, pomegranates could produce considerably better returns than the citrus, almonds, and pistachios that occupied most of our acreage. While the market for pomegranates was still tiny, it was growing.

The meeting wasn't about marketing pomegranates. It was about creating a market for pomegranate juice. There were several problems that made this unlikely. For starters, only about one in ten Americans said they were familiar with pomegranates, and fewer than half of that group said they had eaten one in the past year. So we weren't exactly responding to pent-up demand. We were talking about producing juice from a fruit that the overwhelming majority of Americans didn't know existed.

But we were responding to *something*. In 1996, we had begun funding medical research into the health properties of pomegranates, inspired, in part, by centuries of myth and folklore about the pomegranate's medicinal virtues. For centuries, different parts of the fruit—arils, rind, juice, bark—have been used to treat a wide range of ailments. In his *Natural History*, written in the first century, Pliny the Elder stated that "the branches of the pomegranate keep away snakes, the little buds . . . neutralize the stings of scorpions, and the fruit is in request for easing the nausea of women with child."

The Greek physician Dioscorides cited pomegranates as a treatment for ulcers, earaches, and, according to one early, unintentionally comic, translation, "griefs in ye nosthrills." The tenth-century Italian physician Shabbetai Donnolo recommended pomegranates not only for earaches but for laryngitis, as well.

Elsewhere, pomegranates were a symbol of fertility and wealth. In the *Odyssey*, Homer wrote of pomegranates in the gardens of the kings of Phrygia and Paecia. Maximilian I, the Holy Roman Emperor, adopted the pomegranate as his personal emblem and held one in his left hand as he sat for a 1519 portrait by Albrecht Dürer. Jewish folklore maintains there are 613 luscious ruby arils inside the pomegranate, one for each good deed to be accomplished in a lifetime.

The Koran advises against acting "extravagantly" when the pomegranate has borne fruit. In the Bible, the Song of Solomon identifies love with pomegranates in bloom. But the pomegranate was also used to animate less amorous passions. When Queen Isabella (the troublemaker who started the Inquisition) launched her conquest of the Muslim south of Spain, she vowed to take Andalusia like a ripe pomegranate—"one seed at a time."

While the fruit wasn't well known in the United States, it had clearly cut an impressive swath across much of the world, establishing an honored place in cultures as far away as India and China. We figured you didn't get a reputation like that—across different eras, lands, and cultures—unless there was at least a little bit of truth to the stories. Still, we had no idea what this bundle of myth, superstition, genuine folk medicine, and ancient wisdom would yield in terms of real health benefits. Was there anything here that could be documented by real science?

The early research, conducted at UCLA, UC Davis, Rutgers, the Technion Institute in Israel, and other leading institutions, was jaw-dropping. Among the first findings: pomegranate juice inhibits inflammation and pain. In addition, pomegranates turn out to be astonishingly rich in antioxidants, which inhibit oxidation in the body that can damage cells. Indeed, pomegranates are significantly richer in antioxidants than red wine, green tea, or just about anything else known to humankind. In addition, the fruit was shown to reduce arterial plaque and factors leading to atherosclerosis. Subsequent studies suggested that pomegranates have a powerful effect against prostate cancer.

In short, the news on the health benefits of pomegranates started off great. Then it proceeded to get better and then astound. One glitch: to get the full health benefits of this magnanimous fruit, you would have to eat it virtually by the pound—consuming two and a half whole pomegranates per day. Pomegranates are hard to open, and when they splatter—well, who has that many raincoats? It was all too impractical. Despite the emerging profile of the pomegranate as nature's great gift, folks would never be able to consume enough of them to get a daily dose. Unless, of course, they consumed pomegranates in the form of a juice. This might sound like a reasonable solution, but trying to get consistent, high-quality juice from a pomegranate crop is not easy.

We grow the Wonderful variety of pomegranates. When you combine Wonderfuls with the soil and climate of the San Joaquin Valley, you produce the tastiest, sweetest pomegranates in the world. But even under these ideal conditions, pomegranates are fickle. They have to be coaxed off the vine by hand. If the fruit is squeezed too hard, extracting the maximum juice, it bites back—producing a harsh, bitter aftertaste. If you don't squeeze enough juice, well, you'll pretty quickly go broke.

We literally spent years experimenting with juicers and applications. Eventually, we had to invent our own pressing technology. Then we had to figure out how to feed the presses more than a million pieces of fruit each day, which required a maze of conveyors and elevators operating with all the precision of a Broadway chorus line.

Even now, there are significant variations in sugar and acidity from one year's pomegranate crop to the next, and they even differ from orchard to orchard. Each season, we recalibrate the entire juicing process to accommodate the mood of the latest harvest.

I remember walking the orchards one hot afternoon in early fall. Using a jerry-rigged champagne press right there in the field, one of the farmers made a batch of fresh juice for me. When it's done right, pomegranate juice produces not merely a specific taste but a full sensory explosion in the mouth. It's tart yet sweet, heady with a robust, complex mouth feel. It has more in common with a fine Burgundy than with lesser juices like grape, pear, or apple.

The foundation of the juice business is essentially waste

management. (It's a lovely turn of phrase—makes you want to toast your health.) In practice, it makes a virtue of necessity. When grapes or apples are grown, for instance, there are always those unfortunate little specimens that just aren't pretty enough to pass the fresh-fruit threshold. What do you do with them? Squeeze them. Under that slightly bruised, discolored apple skin may be the sweetest, most delicious fruit of the tree. In the spirit of making lemonade from lemons, growers manage their unsightly "waste" by transforming it into juice.

IN THE CLUTTERED CHAOS of Stewart's conference room, the window ledges and conference table were strewn with various juice bottles, nearly three dozen in all, each labeled with its generally dubious contents. Around the long wooden table was a collection of cheerless marketing consultants and somber executives who no doubt wondered what I was doing in their midst. I had run into similar gentlemen (there was not a dame among them) in the past. I was familiar with their marketing gospel and commandments, their "thou musts" and "thou shalt nots."

The marketing gurus understood the challenge; in addition to the fact that few Americans had ever heard of a pomegranate, the fruit has a truncated harvest season (it begins in October and lasts less than three months) and a high retail price. A complicating factor was presumed to be a massive overproduction problem stemming from all the acreage my "crazy" husband had planted.

The team leader began with the confidence of a man who knows the one true path. "We will mix pomegranate juice with filler juices like white grape and pear and compete with those juices in the 'shelf-stable' aisles of the supermarket," he announced in what sounded to me like a eulogy for our unlaunched product. Visions of hideous, gasoline-type plastic jugs danced in my head.

He had already figured out the appropriate juice mix, saying "We won't be able to use more than ten percent pomegranate juice because it is too expensive. More would throw us out of our competitive advantage." I believe at this point I started to squirm.

The mention of "competitive advantage" was required by the setting. After all, we were contemplating launching a business. Without competitive advantage, there's no business. But pomegranate juice has only two such advantages, and they're very distinct. The first is its sensuous taste; the second, its remarkable health benefits. It seemed the plan was to dilute each of these powerful advantages by a full 90 percent. He was proposing to load diluted, adulterated pomegranate juice onto the nation's supermarket shelves next to similarly adulterated junk juice and simply hope for the best. While this well-meaning expert droned on, I imagined walking up the supermarket aisle in a rolling sea of red—from Hi-C to Welch's. The only way to stand out in that crowd would be to color our juice DayGlo lime— except Gatorade had already done that.

Summoning an inner strength usually reserved for saying "no" to pumpkin pie on Thanksgiving, I held my tongue through a couple hours of strategic marketing jargon as these gurus extolled the benefits of adding still more volume to the supermarket's red sea, despite an already perilously high tide. Then the tasting began.

Much of what America consumes when it buys prepackaged juices has misleading messaging. If the package says "Cranberry-Grape 100% Juice," chances are it's loaded with a little cranberry and lots of grape, pear, apple, and other content chosen solely for economy's sake. If the label says something like "Cranberry-Raspberry Drink," you might as well just pour yourself a Coca-Cola, because the main ingredients are almost certainly water and high-fructose corn syrup—a ubiquitous recipe that has done much to advance the cause of obesity over the past three decades.

Some people can sing. Some can draw. I can taste. I mean *really* taste. Stewart used to show me off at wine tastings, where, blindfolded, I could name the wine I was drinking and the year it was produced. I never imagined there would be a payoff to this particular talent—beyond the amusement of my husband and a few friends. My memory of that delicious taste of pomegranate juice in the orchard was still very fresh in my mind; I knew what pomegranate juice *should* taste like. The various forms of pomegranate pretenders that crossed my palate during this meeting could not have been more of an affront to that memory.

Various concoctions were pushed across the table, but their basic composition was the same: 10 percent pomegranate juice, 80 percent filler juices, and a 10 percent bonus of exotic flavoring. These included watermelon (delicious if you like Kool-Aid), lemon-lime (gag me), Hawaiian Tropical (whatever that means); they ran the dreadful gamut of phony fruit flavorings common in cheap candy and awful soda. The presentation proceeded with all the excitement of a chemistry final.

It was not my intention to insult the marketing team. And I doubt, given their supreme confidence, that I could have insulted them even if I had wanted to. But like most people in business, I had been in these types of meetings before, and I have seen people hold their tongues because they were intimidated by know-it-alls holding forth, because they didn't feel confident enough to challenge them or comfortable enough to upset the apple juice cart.

But I also knew that Stewart would soon turn to me and pose a question. And when he did, I told him the truth.

"What do you think?" he asked.

"I think you're crazy," I said.

"Yeah, I know," he countered. "But what about the pomegranate marketing strategy?"

There are always several different ways to make the same point. Whether the discussion is corporate or marital (or in this case a little of both), it's usually better to take a delicate path, one of constructive criticism delivered in a polite, gentle, and supportive framework. Someday, I promise, I will honor that universal truth. On this day, I dropped the velvet glove and picked up the sledgehammer.

"It's wrong," I said. "Just plain wrong."

"This is the real deal," I said to Stewart, "a gift from God—perhaps the healthiest natural product on the planet. If you water it down with filler juices, you water down its effectiveness. And if you do that, what do you have left?"

This was greeted with the raised eyebrows and sideways glances that welcome the loud and inebriated to an art lecture. The marketing team was not amused, but I had been asked to give my opinion, and I was not going to coat it in sugar—or corn syrup. Sometimes I think I know something and feel an annoying little quiver in my gut that tells me that maybe it isn't so. This was not one of those times. Despite all the challenges involved in creating this product—and at this point, I knew only a fraction of them—I wasn't burdened by self-doubt. My confidence never wavered. Why? Because I knew these were rubies in the orchard; pomegranates had real value.

Pure and unadulterated, this juice was not only delicious; it had the power to help heal people. It was health in a bottle. People needed pomegranate juice in their lives (even if they didn't know it yet), and I knew they would pay what it was worth.

Of course, there would be marketing challenges; but marketing is all about overcoming those challenges. If you have a product with intrinsic value, you can find a way to prevail. Besides, the fact that Starbucks could charge nearly $4.00 for a latte bolstered my resolve. A daily dose of pomegranate juice would cost less than that—and instead of giving you the three o'clock jitters, it would give you health.

"We know that pomegranates are very expensive to grow and harvest, and we know that hardly anyone knows what a pomegranate is," I agreed. "But I don't consider those reasons to go the way of all packaged goods. I see those reasons as the inspiration to create a new category of food."

I wrote **POM** on a piece of paper and passed it to Stewart. "Here is the name of your product. The heart will immediately tell them it's heart-healthy. We'll sell it in the refrigerated section of the produce department, and I'll design a bottle for you that will embody the spirit of this new food category."

I had made my case. It was time to sit back and wait for the usual chorus of naysaying to begin. I wasn't disappointed. Although, in the end, it was less a chorus and more like variations on the theme of *Mission: Impossible*. The meeting ended inconclusively, with the various junk-juice concoctions still littered about the room.

That evening, Stewart told me he understood what I had been saying in the conference room. What's more, he was willing to believe it might work. Then, with the same tone he uses when he asks, "What's for dinner?" he said, "Why don't you take over the business? You seem to have a vision for it."

When will I learn to keep my mouth shut?

————

I HAVE ALWAYS BEEN the marketer in the family. Stewart runs the shop, figures out the financing and margins, and hires the core executive team. I work on building the brands. A few people have very kindly called me a marketing genius. Naturally, I never tire of hearing that, but it isn't true.

I know what and who I am—and I am not a genius. I am, however, smart, disciplined, and hardworking. So far, that has proved to be enough to create a life in marketing that has often been thrilling. I have learned over and over, however, that good marketing for bad products inevitably leads to a dead end. I have been down that road myself, and I've watched others travel it. But I've also seen good products languish because they were poorly positioned, misunderstood by the very people responsible for promoting them.

For me, every marketing campaign begins with the same question: What is the intrinsic value of the product or service? When I talk about "rubies in the orchard," that's what I mean. Where does the value reside? And how can we coax it out and communicate it to consumers in a creative and cost-effective way?

> Every marketing campaign begins with the same question: What is the intrinsic value of the product or service?

Before you are able to convince consumers of the value of something, you have to be able to convince yourself. If it's not immediately apparent to you, it won't be to them either. That's where research comes in. Before we squeezed our first pomegranate into a bottle, I wanted to know everything there was to know about this fruit—and then some. I studied scientific data and interviewed doctors who were conducting tests. I delved into history, art, and literature. And I ate more pomegranates in more ways than you can imagine.

It wasn't enough for *me* to be passionate about the product I intended to bring to market. Just because you own a company (or an idea) doesn't mean your colleagues or employees (or spouse!) will follow you blindly into the marketplace. You must market ideas to your team before you can market them to the public. A lack of faith is deadly. Everyone needs to be a believer.

For me, the hardest sell is usually Stewart. He always plays devil's advocate against both sides of every argument. Grrrr! But in the case of 100 percent pure pomegranate juice, he saw the same great promise I did and was on board from the start. My first COO, however, wasn't quite so enthused. He was extremely capable and uniquely qualified to run the business with me, but he spent the better portion of his working day hunched over his computer, analyzing financial models that proved beyond doubt that there was just no way this juice business was going to work.

Business is often viewed as the realm of science and industry, of logistics, numbers, and cold, hard, irreducible facts. But like every other part of life, it's also a matter of faith. We see the proof of this every day, all around us. Talented people who lack faith in themselves or their mission fail, while people with less talent and more faith succeed. Bill Gates turned his back on a bright future the day he dropped out of Harvard. Ted Turner borrowed irresponsibly to buy the underperforming Atlanta television station that he built into CNN.

We all know these as great business stories. But more often, they're not business stories at all. That college dropout from Seattle didn't have a business. He had faith. The cowboy entrepreneur with a plan for a twenty-four-hour news channel didn't have a financial plan that any sober executive would find compelling (his competitors thought it was a joke). What he had was faith.

> Business . . . is a matter of faith.

Building brands is, first and foremost, not about numbers. It is about value and people. If, on the marketing side, you have people with faith in the value of the brand, you can communicate and extend that faith to consumers. If even a small core of consumers begins to have faith in your product, you've got the building blocks of a winner.

In the beginning, I was having a hard time building a team and getting the business off the ground. Without the COO's emotional investment in the project, it was hard to get emotional investment from others. Every time we tried to take flight, something, some nagging doubt, some form of disbelief, would drag us back down to Earth.

We had so many other hurdles to overcome—operations problems, computer issues, and, two years running, a smaller crop than we had anticipated. (Demand outdistanced our supply by 300 percent, which may sound like good news, but, I can assure you, it was not.)

Gaining traction for a new brand is hard enough under the best circumstances. Without the level of emotional investment you get when people really believe in something, it's just about impossible. So before you spend a nickel to convince a consumer of anything, make sure you've convinced yourself and the people in your own office.

A month after that meeting in the conference room, as I prepared to show my marketing plan to Stewart and his sales force, I still had faith, although the facts of my particular situation were not all that encouraging. I was driving my brilliant designer, Bryan Honkawa, crazy.

I wanted something that would make POM's bottle as distinctive as its content. I didn't know what it was, but I was pretty sure I would recognize it when I saw it. Knowing how important it was to me, Bryan was in the process of producing about 100 different designs, hoping one of them would be "it."

There are many points in business when you need to compromise—either with your colleagues or with a stubborn reality. There are also a few areas that are so critically important that compromise is fatal. To me, the design of the POM bottle belonged in the latter category.

Why did the POM bottle have to stand out? If you've ever walked the aisles of a supermarket, you already know the answer. The run-of-the-mill American supermarket is

50,000 square feet of visual noise featuring nearly 50,000 SKUs (stock keeping units)—about one SKU for every square foot. It's an eye-popping cacophony of bold, bright colors and logos—all screaming for attention. Junk cereals and snack foods clamor to catch your child's wandering eye. Soft drinks scream out in bold reds, blazing oranges, and bright greens, high-fructose heralds of the artificial sweet life.

Many of these products benefit from marketing budgets in the tens of millions. How could we compete with them and distinguish our product from theirs if we all looked alike and they had all the advertising money? We couldn't.

We had come this far by focusing on the fundamentals, going deeper and deeper inside our product to understand its intrinsic value. Everything we needed to know was there inside the pomegranate. We had to resist the temptation to "think outside the box."

I know that's become a fashionable cliché in recent years, but it's just about always wrong. The answers are not outside the box—they're inside. They're inherent in whatever task you've undertaken, whatever product you want to market.

When I walked in to review the bottle designs, the answer was immediately apparent. It was so obvious, in fact, that I would have had the same instant response if Bryan had offered me 10,000 designs to choose from. The solution, of course, was fundamental, intrinsic to the pomegranate itself, inherent in the product we were bringing to market. Among the many choices was a shape that resembled one pomegranate on top of another. The bottle was derived from the juice's natural container. How perfect.

> **The answers are not outside the box—they're inside.**

There was just one little problem. Every packaging engineer said this bottle couldn't be manufactured in plastic (our first choice) and it was near to impossible in glass. Sure, an artisan glassblower could easily make *one*, but we needed millions. Bottle manufacturers are used to creating simple, cylindrical shapes at very high speeds. Shaping molten glass into a delicate pomegranate crown while spitting out thousands of units per minute simply wasn't in their repertoire.

The unique shape of the POM bottle also made printing on it difficult. It took a number of painful adjustments to figure that one out. Finally, filling the bottles with juice in a high-speed filling facility proved to be a shattering experience—a bit like industrialized bumper cars. Bottles constantly collided. With typical, straight-walled bottles, this bumping isn't a big deal. We solved the problem of our crashing bottles by creating a barely perceptible straight edge on the outside of each sphere.

At each hurdle, it might have made sense to throw up our hands, admit defeat, and do what so many experts were telling us to do: get a normal bottle. The only catch to that "follow the rule" consensus was that we weren't going to spend tens of millions of dollars to market our product. That beautiful, distinct bottle was going to have to carry part of the marketing load. It was integral to the product and too important to the brand to simply let it go.

We climbed—and sometimes crawled—over the obstacles. When I finally made my presentation to Stewart and his group, the marketing gang had the gung ho spirit of children forced to eat Brussels sprouts.

- "No one will ever pay $3.50 for a bottle of juice."
- "No one wants a glass bottle."
- "Men won't buy POM with a heart on it."

Oh, well. At least Stewart continued to stand by my vision. We may have been sailing on a sea of doubt, but there was still plenty of faith aboard ship.

CHAPTER 2

Selling Ice Sculptures to Eskimos

I didn't start out focused on value. I'm not sure I would have seen the rubies in the orchard at the beginning of my career or understood why it was so important to nurture them. I was a product of the time and place into which I was born. Generally speaking, that meant the burgeoning consumer landscape of mid-twentieth century America. More particularly, it meant the household of one natural-born Philadelphia huckster.

My father, Jack Harris, was always selling. He couldn't help himself. He was a movie distributor on the East Coast with high hopes of realizing a Hollywood dream of his own. The 1950s were a tough time for distributors. Movie houses were closing across the country, felled by that rectangular miracle that was swiftly conquering the American living room. As a distributor, he sold movies before they were seen, even by him, which required an ability to paint a lively picture not only of the riveting drama-to-be on-screen, but of the crowds that would leave their televisions behind to line up outside the cinema. Dad sold an idea.

And me? I was Daddy's little girl. Little was the operative word: at the age of four, I wore a size one. I talked my way onto a regular role on *The Horn & Hardart Children's Hour*, a live weekly television show sponsored by the king of the automat—essentially a wall of vending machine boxlets from which your food was dispensed. I couldn't sing or dance, but at the audition I took command of the stage and talked. Man, did I talk. They liked me. I was the littlest stand-up comedienne they'd ever seen—so short they thought I was sitting down.

I liked the feeling of power—and the boost to my four-year-old ego—derived from owning center stage. My father, who had encouraged my television career over my mother's objections, coached me on my skit every Thursday, and come Sunday morning I went into the studio and delivered.

One week, my father didn't get back from a business trip in time to go over the routine with me. When the show began that weekend, I was unprepared. I fumbled my lines and began to cry—on live television. When I got back to my house, the neighborhood kids added insult to televised injury by taunting me about my very public tears, an opportunity for which they had been waiting months. A lesson was seared into my very young consciousness: I would never again be unprepared for a presentation. Never.

That era in America was a time of unprecedented

plenty. The consumer society that had begun to take root at the turn of the century had stalled in the Depression and been diverted to military ends during the world wars. But in the wide-open economic expansion that followed World War II, not even a lengthy war in Korea could stop American consumerism from roaring forward.

Harvard historian Lizabeth Cohen, who documented this land of plenty in A Consumer's Republic, noted that between 1946 and 1956, the national output of goods and services doubled. New-car sales quadrupled during the same period, and the percentage of American families that owned a refrigerator rose from 44 percent in 1940 to 80 percent by 1950. Before the end of the 1950s, John Kenneth Galbraith would publish The Affluent Society, analyzing (sometimes tartly) the unprecedented riches of a nation in which mechanical conveniences—and television, too!—were suddenly commonplace.

Consumption became culture in America, a vast machinery of marketing and salesmanship geared up to meet growing consumer appetites as well as to inspire desires, in Galbraith's words, "that previously did not exist." Personal credit expanded to accommodate the new American Way of easy monthly payments. Keeping up with the Joneses grew to rival baseball as the great American pastime. Feeding—and creating—consumer appetites became a huge business.

I threw my lot in with this Great American Selling Machine when I was still in my teens. My father had recently produced a horror movie destined to become a B-movie classic: *The Blob.* He wasted no time in moving us to southern California, where he adopted a lifestyle befitting a newly minted Hollywood mogul. We quickly had two Rolls-Royces in the driveway and a more or less permanent sense that we should enjoy the good times while they lasted, because financial doom was probably just around the next corner. My father is charming, gregarious, and loads of fun, and he *loved* to spend money—at least on *some* things.

Having long dreamed of being an artist, I was delighted when, after graduating from high school, I was accepted by the best art school in Los Angeles. Unfortunately, my father adamantly refused to pay the tuition. With a house in Beverly Hills and a pair of Rolls-Royces in the drive, I couldn't exactly plead poverty and beg the college for financial assistance. So for a year I ended up at a city college, where I was bored and frustrated.

My dreams of being a fine artist were all too easily dashed. The real artists I knew would do whatever they had to do, including living in poverty, to pursue their art. Even at a young age, I wanted the security and independence that I knew money could bring. I gave up on art and got a job at a dress shop instead. For the next forty years, I would never bother with long-range planning again. What was the point? Instead, I learned to go with whatever flow life provided, including the occasional rip tide.

I also learned quickly that, like the backslapping, gladhanding kings of sales, I, too, could "sell ice to Eskimos." Selling was like breathing to me; it came so naturally I didn't have to think much about it. Eventually, I discovered it was even better to sell the Eskimos ice *sculptures*—and charge a premium for the value added. But in the beginning, I sold dresses to women with closets already chock full of them, and I sold them like mad. They were frequently returned by customers who were also mad. After checking their new purchases in their mirrors at home, without the musical accompaniment of my sales spiel, they discovered they had made a big mistake.

Returned merchandise doesn't make for a very strong foundation in retailing. The shop owners complained constantly about the lack of business. To help them out, I drew enchanting little female characters that embodied the mode of the times. Then I worked up headlines and text to accompany my illustrations. The owners placed these homespun ads in the local papers.

It worked. Customers came in talking about the charming advertising and wanting to see what we had to offer. The owners were only too happy to take me off the merry-go-round of sales-followed-by-returns and keep me in the back room creating advertising instead. I was happier, too. I had found something that made use of both my natural design sense and my precocious marketing savvy. I was no longer a salesgirl; I was in the early stages of becoming a marketer.

Local newspaper reps taught me how to size an ad and set type. That's when I first learned a lesson that would be crucial throughout my career: you get a lot further in life by showing what you *don't* know and asking for help than you do by pretending to know it all. I have seen very accomplished people make big mistakes by succumbing to their insecurities and not asking questions when they should have.

> You get a lot further in life by showing what you don't know and asking for help than you do pretending you know it all.

I soon left the dress shop for a job at Sunset House, a mail-order company that sold a wide array of what might charitably be called useless gadgets. The Sunset House catalog offered one-stop shopping for everything you didn't need and likely would never use: automatic back scratchers, Sea-Monkeys, fallout shelter supplies, tie-dye kits. Sure, it was junk, but I was happy to work for its in-house ad agency. The experience, like most early experience, proved to be extremely valuable.

Sunset House ads consisted of far too little information about far too many products crammed into far too small a space. The magazine ads appeared on a grid, usually divided into nine boxes. Compressed inside each box was a tiny picture of a product, a headline, and some body copy. Success depended almost entirely on the allure of the headline, which offered the only, albeit slim, chance of grabbing a reader's attention. A production artist taught me how to lay out an ad and how to write headlines and copy that were attention-grabbing, yet sufficiently concise to fit the space.

On the side, I started freelancing for local shops, taking my growing portfolio from store to store. Eventually, I acquired enough freelance work to leave Sunset House and open my own little agency, Lynda Limited. I was nineteen. Around the same time, I got married.

I had no particular philosophy (let alone vision) about what I was doing in life or in business. I just loved advertising—I still do—and I was going with the flow. I can still recall the brilliant ads for Volkswagen and Alka-Seltzer and the now-defunct Braniff Airways. Braniff paired artist Andy Warhol and boxer Sonny Liston in one ad. The combination was so thoroughly bizarre that you couldn't take your eyes off them. I thrilled to the cutting-edge ad work of Mary Wells and Doyle Dane Bernbach. At that age, I loved everything about advertising—even the deceit. I had a lot to learn.

The turning point for my business was a direct-mail piece I developed for a charming potpourri of a shop in the San Fernando Valley called The Store. I had a ridiculously low budget for the job, so I got on the phone with the printing house to price paper. After every price quote I would respond, "Too expensive. What do you have that's cheaper?"

As it turned out, their cheapest paper cost more than my entire budget.

"Isn't there any kind of paper cheaper than that?" I pleaded. "Even if you don't carry it?"

The only thing the printer could think of was brown kraft paper—the kind supermarkets use to pack your groceries. "No photos," the printer advised, "and any color of ink as long as it's black."

I made do. Since typesetting was too expensive, I hand-lettered the entire thing and drew all the illustrations. On the outside of the self-mailer (I couldn't afford envelopes), a pair of eyes peered through antique wire-framed glasses. The headline read, "Look inside and be stupefied."

Believe it or not, that was a breakthrough. The piece went out to a list of names collected from friends, acquaintances, and local shoppers. Then I left for the East Coast to show my grandparents my new baby boy. When I returned, my husband handed me a long list of messages from potential new clients.

While other kids my age were smoking pot, discovering sex (as if no one ever had before), and grumbling about the establishment, I was a full-time working mother with a load of responsibilities both at home and at the office. By twenty-three, I had another baby boy and a growing business.

I developed offbeat approaches that would serve me well in later, larger businesses. I had a sense of humor, which was communicated in my work, some of which was not easily forgotten.

In one case, a young swimsuit manufacturer came to me with a real dilemma. He was hitting Market Week in New York for the first time. He was smart enough to realize that advertising in *Women's Wear Daily* would get him attention and help his business grow, but he was also worried about competitors getting an early look at his designs.

"You have complete creative license," he told us, a beautiful phrase that rang like a hymn in our ears, "as long as you don't show the swimsuits in the ads."

"You're kidding," I replied.

"No, this industry is vicious," he said. "If you show the product, by the time I land in New York, I'll see my designs in everyone else's showrooms."

He was a dream account, with the guts to really go for it. So we did. We created a jaw-dropping double page ad featuring the "Little Nothing" suit—consisting of a nude model in a Rubenesque pose with fruit nestled in all the right places. Our client got a front-page story in New York's *Daily News* during Market Week, his showroom was jammed and his ultimate dream came true; he sold his business to Jantzen a few years later.

My renamed agency, Lynda Sinay Advertising, had a dozen employees, a larger office, and some very nice clients. Then I did two things that jeopardized everything for which I had worked so hard.

There was a fellow who kept asking me out to lunch and suggesting that we merge our businesses. I reminded him that he was a freelancer—he *had* no business. He insisted that if we teamed up, he could bring in a big account. Besides, he was a pretty good creative director, certainly a better one than I could afford.

I had an uncomfortable feeling about this from the beginning. I didn't like the guy, but I convinced myself that

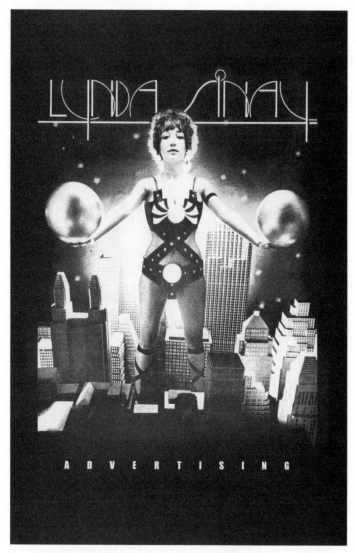

Lynda Sinay agency promotion poster from 1970.

it was business, not personal. After all, I wasn't *marrying* him. I suggested, "Let's work together for six months and see how it goes. If we like each other, we'll put your name on the door." He agreed.

There was a phrase making its way around feminist political circles in those days: "The personal is political." Well, guess what? Business is personal, too—and anyone who forgets that does so at her peril.

For the first six months, the relationship was lovely. He brought in the big account, and we staffed up to service it. Then, a few days after the six-month deadline, with his name now accompanying mine on our joint business cards, he started coming late to the office. As the weeks progressed, he took two-hour lunches, then whole days off to play golf.

Our office was not known for leisure; we were more sweatshop than country club. I worked at least six days a week and frequently seven. In that environment, his work ethic was an affront to everyone in the agency. Also, he had convinced himself that I found him wildly desirable, which led to an ugly late-night office encounter.

He quit and took the big account with him. The day he left was one of the longest of my life. First, there was a staff celebration—they disliked him as much as I did. Then my assistant and I closed the doors and ordered pizza and extra cigarettes. We analyzed all the accounts and what it would take for me to keep the shop open—and keep my newly expanded workforce in paychecks—while I hustled to replace the lost revenue. By 6:00 a.m., we had the answer: $20,000—that would be about $130,000 today.

I went home, got the kids ready for school, and then dressed to the nines. I met the manager of a local bank, who gave me the loan I needed to keep the business afloat. I repaid it in half the allotted time and soon welcomed back the big AWOL account. The client had quickly figured out who had really been doing the work and was eager to return.

But all was not well. I was twenty-four years old and looked forty-two. While my business was flourishing, my personal life was crumbling. My eldest child had been diagnosed with serious neurological problems, and I was in the midst of divorcing my husband, who decided to get back at me by withholding child support. Then came recession, and things began to unravel at work, too.

Between the Vietnam War, assassinations, radical violence, street crime, and racial, cultural, and generational clashes dividing the country, things weren't really going too well anywhere. I began doing some occasional work for the antiwar movement—creating posters and such. And my new boyfriend introduced me to his friend, a nice man named Daniel Ellsberg, who had previously worked at the Pentagon and at RAND, the government-funded think tank that did a vast amount of strategic analysis for the military. Dan, who had turned against the war, asked for a favor. Could he use my Xerox 812 photocopy machine on nights and weekends? I said sure. What could be the harm in that?

So at odd hours, Dan copied a trove of documents not very discreetly labeled "Top Secret." My favorites were the

Press from the Pentagon Papers trial: Time *magazine and (left to right)* L.A. Daily News, Chicago Tribune, New York Post, *and* Los Angeles Times.

carbon copies labeled "Eyes Only." Dan said the documents were so important they could stop the war in Vietnam. It seemed like a good idea at the time.

Like the country, I soon found myself in very deep trouble. I stopped dating Dan's friend, and Dan and his wife, Pat, moved back to Cambridge. Some months later, however, I read a story about the "Pentagon Papers" in the press. The whole thing had a familiar ring to it. Before long, Dan and my old boyfriend were implicated. A few days later, at 5:30 p.m. on a gloomy June afternoon in 1971, two FBI agents knocked at my door. They handed me a subpoena to appear before a grand jury the next day.

For the next two years, I was pursued by a very nasty prosecutor and my life was dominated by the Pentagon Papers case. I spiraled into debt and had to let all my employees go. Eventually, the case against Dan was dismissed and the cloud of potential prosecution lifted. I crawled out of a very dark place.

Not so the nation. The misery of Vietnam was soon compounded by the shock of Watergate. Together, they took the air out of the country's sails. The war ended and Watergate passed, but the cynicism lingered—a deeper, more abiding cynicism than America had ever known.

Toward the very end of my ad agency career, I did a great marketing campaign for a restaurant. I designed the space, planned the menu, even outfitted the staff. The client was delighted, and I was proud of the job I had done. There was only one catch: the food was awful. That was it for me. I could invent the advertising, create the marketing, and design the look, but what good was it if the product was junk?

> What good are advertising, marketing, and design if the product is junk?

I was tired of the game. I just didn't want to sell ice to Eskimos anymore. Maybe I could sell them heaters.

CHAPTER 3

———————

Taking Root in the Flower Business

Somewhere between my advertising firm spiraling down and the government hounding me for my tenuous connection to the Pentagon Papers, my personal life took a very sharp turn. After my divorce, I found myself a single mom with two small boys. Having married at nineteen, I was single essentially for the first time in my life. After my first out-of-the-box relationship (with the fellow who had introduced me to Dan Ellsberg) ended, a man who was on a board of directors with me kept telling me about a brilliant young businessman who wanted to meet me. He was in the janitorial business.

"Sounds thrilling," I thought (and may even have said).

When Stewart and I finally met—I went to his office because he was allegedly interested in my advertising skills—he made fun of my outfit. I thought he was cute but a bit of a jerk. He kept pursuing meetings, though, frequently after hours at my house. He was as brilliant as advertised, and he had great business insights. Besides, he was growing on me. When I asked him if he was ever going to give me the account, he responded, "I really want to have a meaningful relationship with you." I never got the account. But I sure got the business.

Stewart eventually sold that janitorial business to ITT for half stock and half cash. The stock doubled by the time he could divest it, and with that bankroll we began acquiring agricultural land. Over the years, we have bought many companies and sold a few. We discovered early on that we are operating people. We love running businesses and don't like selling them if they meet our expectations. We are in it for the long haul.

Whenever we make an acquisition, Stewart's mantra is always the same: "The management is good. I'll let them run the business and it won't take any time from me at all." (Notice he doesn't say, "It won't take any time from *you*.") The first few times I heard this, I actually believed him, but leaving well enough alone is not what entrepreneurs do, and every business has room for improvement. Some, of course, have more room than others—and ours seem to have more room for improvement than Britney Spears's mothering skills.

In late 1979, we purchased Teleflora, a struggling flower delivery service that was a ninety-eight-pound weakling in the market, overmatched by the brawnier FTD. Unfortunately, this was no time for business weaklings. The economy was sputtering, and the great oil shock of the late 1970s would soon produce record gasoline prices and long lines at service stations. FTD was actually a co-op owned by the florists themselves. When given a choice between using our delivery service or a service they owned themselves, there wasn't much doubt about which way they would turn.

Yet the florists were also the gatekeepers. Customers couldn't tell the difference between one floral wire delivery service and another; they just hoped the florist would complete the delivery across town or across the country. It was a leap of faith.

Teleflora's president came with the deal. He was a swell guy, an old-school, slap-on-the-back guy from the white-loafer set. He had come from a top job at one of the world's most successful companies and was part of the consortium that sold us the company. He wore a button that read "Assume Nothing." It was good advice, especially as it related to him. It seemed his idea was to take the job at Teleflora to semiretire, letting the company drift toward its inevitable fate while he endured lengthy rounds of golf. When he begged me to become head of marketing, it occurred to me that he might have asked me because an extended search to fill the post with an outside executive might have interfered with his tee time.

Within six months, Stewart had become the new president and I was executive vice president of marketing. A short time later, I would become president of Teleflora and enjoy one of the most rewarding work experiences of my life. Having at last moved to the client side of the business, I began to develop the principles of marketing and brand building that would serve me well for the next three decades.

But before I could implement any of my ideas, I first had to learn how to manage—in every sense of the word. I had about three hundred employees, roughly thirty times the maximum number of people I had managed in my small advertising firm. The challenges started soon after I came to Teleflora.

I had developed my first merchandising concept for our florists—a wedding guide and merchandising plan to help brides select flowers and arrangements for their big day. In my typical A-student fashion, the campaign was meticulously thought out, with no detail overlooked.

I presented the plan to Teleflora's field force, the roughly thirty salespeople who were our main points of contact with florists. These were the folks on the front line who sold our services and products to members. Every last one of them was male. Their response to my plan was unanimous—and vicious. In those days, you could be cruel in an office environment, especially to a woman, and this gang spared no contempt or vitriol in dismissing every aspect of my big idea.

I felt the same awful pain I had felt as a child when I was rejected by the Camp Fire Girls, and I responded in pretty much the same way. I retreated to my office, shut the door, and cried. I was rejected by the Camp Fire Girls for a reason I couldn't change: I am Jewish. But as the boss, there was sure something I could do about this.

I could have stoked my hurt and anger into a burning hot coal—then roared back at my insolent staff with all the hellfire I could muster. But rather than run them over, I knew I was going to have to *win* them over. First, you can't fire your entire sales force. Second, like it or not, I would need their support time and again in order to be successful.

So instead of allowing our antagonism to settle into a pattern of trench warfare, I worked hard to become their buddy. I courted my regional sales managers, cultivated their friendship, and worked for their respect. I made them part of my marketing team and part of management. It wasn't easy.

There were times when I wanted to kill one or another of them, but it was the only way. I was not going to play the victim, nor was I going to sacrifice the business in order to dominate a willful bunch of hard-drinking guys who would have resented every order delivered from on high. In time, I won them over—and in the process I made some good friends.

Listening to them was the key, and I learned a lot from it. They had their war stories, they knew the florists, and even though I eventually knew them too, I wasn't the one battling it out day after day against the giant FTD.

The Internet has drastically changed the wire service business. Back then, Teleflora was basically a clearinghouse handling transactions between one florist and another. Let's say you lived in New York and wanted to send flowers to your aunt in Des Moines. You would contact your local florist, tell them what you wanted, and they would find a florist in Des Moines to create the bouquet and make the delivery. The wire service billed the florist in New York (who had the customer's money) and paid the florist in Des Moines (who delivered the flowers). The two florists paid dues to belong to the service network.

Teleflora had about 7,000 member florists when we purchased the company. FTD had about 18,000. Some florists used both services. The only reason those florists needed two networks was to benefit from the "float" of money they needed to get by. If they overextended their credit with FTD, they could turn to Teleflora. It was like moving from one maxed-out credit card to another.

The florists paid Teleflora dues of $7.00 per month. To Stewart, that didn't sound like a lot of money.

"When is the last time you raised the dues?" Stewart asked the V.P. of sales.

"Three years ago," he replied. "We had so many complaints we never did it again."

"Really? How many is 'so many'?" Stewart wanted to know.

"At least fifty."

"Fifty complaints out of seven thousand members isn't that impressive," Stewart concluded.

Stewart was probably determined to raise the dues regardless. His first big success in business had been with an alarm company he had bought in the late 1960s. The business had taken off after he raised the monthly fee and improved the service. The increase in fees had allowed him to cover the cost of service improvements and still have extra profit left over.

Likewise, the most obvious way to increase profits at Teleflora was to raise dues. We needed to figure out how to add value and how to differentiate ourselves from FTD; without adding value for the extra dues, it was bound to be a short-term plan—possibly a *terminal* plan as far as Teleflora members were concerned. What we needed was that old, reliable pillar of marketing: the Unique Selling Proposition. And we needed it fast.

Since my college career had been measured in months and my interests were focused on art, I had never taken a marketing course. Everything I know about marketing I learned on the job. My lack of education would have stalled a career in nuclear physics, but it never hindered my career in marketing. You can't learn how to be a good marketer from a textbook.

Of course, there are advantages to graduating from a top MBA program, but the truth is that there is only so much you can learn in school. The most important lesson of all is self-taught. Ultimately, marketing is all about listening. If you don't listen and you don't care, you'll never be a good marketer. You want to be the equivalent of a good friend—someone who cares, someone who listens carefully, someone who tries to anticipate another's needs and to meet them or indeed exceed them. The rest—market research, statistical analysis, economics, and finance—are really important tools, but in the end, you have to use all that information to inform your own human instincts. That is where your own sound judgment and the empathy quotient come in; you might say it's where the art meets the science.

> Ultimately, marketing is all about listening. You want to
> be the equivalent of a good friend.

Though I didn't encounter it in a textbook, I was familiar with the concept of the Unique Selling Proposition, or USP. It was pioneered in the 1940s by Rosser Reeves, who was the chairman of Ted Bates & Company, one of the most successful firms in advertising history. I'm sure that marketing textbooks give a more comprehensive analysis, but here's how I gauge whether an attribute or marketing claim rises to the standard of a USP.

Unique Selling Propositions

1. Is it true? The honesty factor is essential.
2. Is it clear, concise, and easy to understand? Keep it simple.
3. Does its unique quality answer a need in the marketplace, whether consumers know it or not? That is your success barometer, because if consumers need it, chances are that you will succeed.

That's all. Pretty basic stuff. Yet it's amazing how often businesspeople forget it.

By the same token, we tend to notice—and reward—businesses that never forget to deliver a Unique Selling Proposition. Given the proliferation of coffee shops, consumers often have a local alternative to Starbucks. Starbucks' early success came from its understanding that it was delivering more than a cup of expensive coffee. It created a carefully calibrated social environment with meticulously selected music and a warm, friendly, and distinctively intelligent atmosphere. The coffee is premium. The experience is premium-plus. Recently Starbucks has lost its focus and become more like a large packaged goods company; growing too fast, slipping on its core values, and driving the business for quarterly earnings instead of long-term sustainability. Bringing the inspired founder, Howard Schultz, back to the helm should help steer the ship back to its course.

Similarly, Lexus has staked its brand on quality and, in the process, redefined quality by raising the bar several notches. What does it sound like when you close the door of a Lexus? Like you've just entered an airtight chamber. From the quiet yet powerful hush of the engine to the accoutrements—leather, wood, glass, and so on—every detail is engineered to join the chorus singing "This is quality."

Differentiating a brand by virtue of a Unique Selling Proposition is just as powerful today as it was in a bygone era. Remember Maxwell House coffee? In a pre-Starbucks era, it promised to purge the acidic, bitter taste that settled to the bottom of the coffee cup. Maxwell House, we were informed, was "good to the last drop."

At Teleflora, a USP was absolutely essential. In the pre-Internet era, consumers phoned or visited a neighborhood florist to make a selection for a gift, so the florist was the gatekeeper—and FTD was like a gated community. We had to figure out a way to pull florists away from their familiar home turf, get them outside the gates, and send orders through the Teleflora network instead of through FTD. Since florists had no incentive to alter their preference for FTD, we needed to give someone else an incentive to demand it: consumers.

In the early 1980s, the U.S. economy had still not recovered. In fact, 1982 ushered in a massive recession. Flowers, then as now, were a luxury, and they were a peculiar luxury—one that died. My research indicated that one reason people were afraid to send flowers was that they didn't know what would show up on the recipient's doorstep. I was desperate for a way not only to differentiate our service from FTD's but to give consumers added value that would inspire them to ask specifically for Teleflora flowers. Then I thought of the container the flowers came in.

Instead of simply sending flowers in a throwaway green glass vase, we could put the flowers in a gift. That way, when the flowers died, the recipients would still have the gift to remind them of the sentiment with which the flowers had been sent. For the price of flowers offered by our competitors, Teleflora would instead provide flowers in a keepsake watering can, a lovely tea cup, or a cookie jar. My concept gave wire customers peace of mind; they knew exactly what would arrive. Teleflora's Unique Selling Proposition was born.

Of course, the real trick was to figure out how to do this and still make a profit. Vendors wanted much more to produce what we called our "keepsakes" than we could afford to pay. Instead, we brought the design in-house, which set the pattern for the way we've done design and advertising work—and just about everything else—ever since. Then we went looking for a way to manufacture, seeking out factories in Far East jungles and remote places with names I can barely pronounce.

We hired a husband-and-wife team—let's call them Ted and Dolly. While not exactly the dream team of corporate etiquette, they turned out to be just what was needed to blaze new territory. Dolly was a whiz at product development ideas and using new materials to make products that looked like a million dollars but cost next to nothing. Ted was a burly guy, straight out of *The French Connection*— with a touch of larceny to drive home the resemblance.

When it came to Ted, you could never be too careful. He looked for every conceivable way to cut corners to get the best possible price. That, in turn, required me to inspect absolutely everything he did to ensure that his sense of thrift wouldn't result in customer complaints—or all of us being shipped off to the penitentiary.

Once, we were creating a "hand-painted" Jell-O mold that, when turned upside down, became a great floral container.

"Ted," I asked, "is this really hand-painted?"

"It sure is," he avowed.

"Well, the words that say 'hand-painted' were put on with a decal," I pointed out. "And it's upside down."

At first our member florists hated the whole idea of the keepsakes. "We are in the flower business, not the container business," they would tell me. They didn't want the added (albeit ever so reasonable) expense, and they didn't like being required to create a preconceived bouquet during holidays.

On one trip to Texas Retail, a huge floral show, I was separated from my team. A group of florists invited me to join them in their van on the way to the next event. It wasn't until after we had all piled in and they had locked the door that I started to sweat. "We want you to get out of the container business," they threatened. I brought out pictures of my soon-to-be-orphaned children and prayed the furious florists would spare me. In time, however, the florists came to an unavoidable conclusion: the keepsakes worked.

We advertised the "flowers in a gift" concept on television and in print and supplied our member florists with posters and direct-mail pieces to send to their customers. Even more important, we sent our design and marketing specialists around the country to teach member florists how to merchandise their shops for each holiday season. An old-fashioned Unique Selling Proposition was the focus of all of our advertising and marketing efforts.

The keepsakes turned the tide for our business. Suddenly, we were going *with* the flow instead of against it.

Business boomed (okay, bloomed). Since we were now adding enormous value to our members' businesses, we were able to grow our network and our profits. From a network of 7,000 florists each paying $7.00 per month we grew to be a network of 21,000 florists paying $140.00 per month. (You do the math.) Today, we are larger than FTD, the erstwhile floral Goliath in whose shadow we once toiled.

We had to transform the company to deliver value. Instead of an also-ran delivery service, we became a marketing and merchandising company for the flower industry. If the rubies are in service, don't go looking elsewhere to nurture value. Go to the essence of the business.

One of the vehicles we used to market to our own members was a magazine we inherited with the company, *The Teleflorist*, which was distributed to all our member florists. It was not a great asset; the art direction was hideous, and the content was meandering and dull. I decided to remake it.

First, I hired a new sales director. I found Diane, an experienced woman who had been working for a very profitable pornography magazine and was willing to take a big pay cut in order to go legit. Then I came up against my next management crucible: the "magazine ladies."

There were a half-dozen women who had run the magazine for years. When I described the changes I envisioned, they sat silently scowling, their arms tightly folded across their chests to form an impenetrable wall of editorial defiance. I wasn't getting anywhere with them, and they were making it abundantly clear that I never would.

My new sales director, late of the pornography indus-try, was not especially subtle. "If I were you," she said, "I'd fire their asses." She'd retained the colorful vernacular of her former job.

I realized I was going to have to do just that. Unlike my earlier experience with the field force, I was getting nowhere with the magazine ladies, who for some reason seemed to think that they had the power to do anything— or more often nothing at all.

Trouble was, I was not the firing kind. When my life was going down the rabbit hole of the Pentagon Papers case and my advertising business was falling apart, I had kept my staff on well beyond any reasonable point. I had gone into debt in order to continue paying their salaries, despite the fact that I didn't have enough work to keep them busy.

I am sure it was traumatic for them, but firing the magazine ladies didn't go over too well with me either. My back went out. My left shoulder and neck were in con-stant, throbbing pain. I was only in my thirties, but my body was a total wreck.

Eventually I learned how to fire people when it's abso-lutely necessary, but it never really gets easier. You just get tough enough as the years go by to handle it, realizing that if you don't get rid of the "deadwood" in your organiza-tion, you hurt the dedicated employees who are the future of your business.

I hired a great editor, Barbara Cady, who raised the magazine's standards and improved its quality. We went on to work with a top designer, Dugald Stermer from San Francisco, who gave the publication a modern, elegant look and feel. *The Teleflorist* was renamed *Flowers&*. It has thrived ever since.

I won an advertising award called the Gold Effie for the keepsake-with-flowers idea. Teleflora's Unique Selling Proposition remains our keepsakes, but the heart of our service is this: each and every bouquet we market has been designed by one of our 21,000 local floral shops and is hand-delivered to the recipient. The other wire services, such as 1-800-Flowers and FTD, do a lot of what we call "drop ship." The flowers are boxed in a warehouse and shipped to addressees. Then it is up to recipients to stop whatever they are doing in the middle of a busy day and arrange the flowers themselves. In addition, our competitors use their services to deliver everything from chocolates to lobsters. Teleflora, on the other hand, focuses only on our florist network, helping them deliver the joy of flowers. (Do I care about this? You bet I do.)

In 1999, the executive board of FTD, which was made up of florists, decided they would sell the co-op. I had come down with a terrible flu and high fever a few days before Stewart and I made the trip to Detroit to make our presentation to purchase the company. I should have stayed home.

In Detroit, the FTD board refused our offer, still viewing Teleflora as their sworn enemy. Instead, they sold FTD to a leveraged-buyout firm, which fired the staff and closed down its beautiful corporate headquarters. FTD is now a publicly traded company and has been led by many different teams of Wall Street management types. They still have plenty of brand equity due to that magical name recognition, but being under Wall Street's thumb is hardly an advantage.

Publicly traded companies throw lots of money into marketing because they want to see the stock price rise. To that end, they must show rapid growth to impress Wall Street. I won't go into my rant about the perils of managing a business for short-term stock price gains rather than the long-term health of the company and employees. Emphasis on the short term almost always comes at the expense of the long term. Just look at the financial quicksand that enveloped Fannie Mae, Freddie Mac, AIG, and most of Wall Street. Merrill Lynch, Lehman Brothers and the rest were riding high, quarter to quarter, on profit from shaky mortgage-backed securities. Denial is a powerful engine, but eventually it runs out of gas. When the fantasy ended, great companies with long and illustrious histories lay in shambles. The contagion spread to every financial capital of the world, destroying the weak and shaking the foundations of the strong. Even Goldman Sachs was forced to end its swashbuckling ways and submit to regulation as a bank holding company. Innocent taxpayers will be paying for the big boys' recklessness for years to come.

But sometimes forest fires are a good thing. Hopefully this debacle will clear out the toxic debris and in the long term bring citizens back to reality about living within their means. It might also give them a healthy skepticism toward the financial markets.

> Emphasis on the short term almost always comes at the
> expense of the long term.

I have been around long enough to have seen several incarnations of the new business model, the new economy, the new visionary geniuses who turn the old ways upside down and reinvent the world of business. "Nothing will ever be the same," we're told.

But it *is* the same. Economies, like societies, are dynamic. They change constantly, but the fundamentals do not. Value is rewarded, while the absence of value, sooner or later, is always exposed and penalized. Every economics lesson, from the tulip craze of the 1600s to the dot-com bubble of 2000, from the construction of the latest pyramid scheme to the collapse of Enron's new-wave energy trading, all confirm the primacy—and constancy—of value.

As you will see in the next chapter, value is real—even when the product itself is a certified, 100 percent fake.

> Value is rewarded, while the absence of value, sooner or
> later, is always exposed and penalized.

CHAPTER 4

The One True Copy of Jackie Kennedy's Real Fake Pearls

Running Teleflora was a dream job. I was in charge of marketing and product development, and, of course, I supervised all my new friends in the sales force, which I had gradually shaped to fit my vision. The business was growing, and so were profits. I had reached a point where I could start delegating some of the work—provided I could let go of a certain nagging perfectionism (which today has a fancy name and a medication regime to go along with it).

My job was fulfilling, and my life with Stewart and the kids had hit a stretch of smooth sailing, about as close to domestic bliss as any family gets. For the first time in my life, things seemed comfortable and easy. With everything going so well, there was naturally only one thing left to do: shake it up.

In 1981, I hired a news clipping service to begin tracking a direct-response company called the Franklin Mint. There were similarities between the Mint and Teleflora. The Mint created unique products, just as we did, only without the flowers. In those days, its products were mostly coins and medallions, a few porcelain vases, and some miniature knickknacks worthy of display in a "free with purchase" vitrine. Unlike Teleflora, the Mint sold its collectibles through direct response, with no middleman between the company and its consumers. It was something I longed to do.

In an effort to replace myself as the New Products Creator at Teleflora, I was looking to hire the right person. The Franklin Mint was located in Philadelphia, where I was originally from. My best friend from childhood had grown up to be a hotshot recruiter, so I sent her into the Mint to find out who was creating their products. In no time at all, Stewart and I were sitting in our garden in California interviewing (or interrogating) the Mint's V.P. of product development. He told me the company was poorly managed and grossly dysfunctional. He also said the Mint might be for sale. We hired that fellow to come to Teleflora, and I went on to persuade Stewart that the Mint might be our next acquisition.

The company was owned by Warner Bros. It had been one of the last acquisitions made by legendary Warner CEO Steve Ross, who loved it. He saw the same potential we did. But he was ill at the time, and his top executives were too busy with their core businesses to pay much attention to this odd direct-marketing business that was miles away in the Pennsylvania countryside.

I had initially thought we might go into competition with the Mint. Stewart always says, "Start-ups are a bitch." Now, having a few in my history, I know he's right. We decided to look into buying it instead. Stewart heard from a Wall Street source that a sale prospectus of the Mint was making the rounds. Eventually, we paid a visit to the Mint's campus, about forty-five minutes outside Philadelphia on the Baltimore Pike. Perched high on a hill, the bucolic landscape included several sprawling buildings with eighty-five acres under roof. It was actually a little city unto itself: Franklin Mint, Pennsylvania.

"You know, the collectibles business is dead. What do you think you are going to bring to the party?" one of the executives asked in his Philadelphia twang. In this person's opinion, the current management was brilliant—and if *they* couldn't make the business work, well, the likes of Stewart and I certainly weren't going to get anywhere.

Steve Ross wasn't eager to sell, but his video business, Atari, was hemorrhaging money and the Warner board was pushing for a sale. In the end, Ross was forced to divest both Atari and the Franklin Mint. The company's sagging stock price had forced decisions based on short-term perceptions rather than long-term value—decisions that might never have been made by a privately held company. Imagine getting rid of the first video game business because "The Street" didn't believe in its long-term viability! It was a sad conclusion for a great business visionary. Steve died of prostate cancer in 1992.

We were more than happy to relieve Warner Bros. of its perceived burden. This would be the end of my brief patch of stress-free living. Stewart and I lived in Beverly Hills, where we've been in the same house for thirty years. That meant quite a commute to the new office in Pennsylvania. We ended up living in a hotel in Philadelphia. Stewart said, "Don't worry about this, we will turn the business around and be back in Beverly Hills in six months. You don't even have to give up your job at Teleflora." Right! For the first three months I almost believed him.

On my first day of work, I asked someone in the Mint's Female Collectibles department about a doll on her shelf.

"Oh, that's Scarlett O'Hara," she sighed, "in her green dress from the barbecue."

"Poor thing is all covered in dust. What happened?"

"Management doesn't believe in Hollywood—it's too riffraff. Conflicts with our image."

Wow. I suddenly knew exactly what I was bringing to the company barbecue.

Even through the dust, I could see that the doll was attractive, intriguing even, with fine features and an unmistakable aura of quality. I called a meeting of sales and sourcing, asking them how many of these little ladies they could produce for me—and how fast.

Overnight, we were in the high-end collectible doll business. Our dolls were based on characters that were both real and fictional, but they all had a built-in following. Our first run of Scarlett generated $35 million in sales. Despite the disdain of the previous management, you will probably not be shocked to discover that Hollywood was enormously popular with our collectors—and profitable.

We went on to do Scarlett in porcelain, in vinyl, in her burgundy Jezebel dress, in her bridal gown, in her widow's weeds, and even in the dress she wore when she delivered Melanie's baby. Our doll collectors knew every nuance of every dress worn in the film.

But our *Gone With the Wind* franchise didn't begin and end with Scarlett. We produced dolls of Mammy, Rhett, Melanie, Prissy, and just about every other character who had ever promenaded, strutted, or crawled across the set of one of the great films of all time. Scarlett O'Hara wasn't just a doll for us. She was an industry.

At the Mint, I learned how to predict and develop winning products. One of the first things I did was banish the word "customer" and replace it with "collector." By referring to the people who bought our products as collectors, we immediately elevated them in the minds of our employees. And we let our collectors know that we understood their passion and respected it.

We nurtured faith in the Franklin Mint brand among a following that eventually grew to eight million collectors worldwide. Our success depended on the interplay of two forces, both of which were at the heart of our value proposition. The first of these was the emotional connection our collectors felt with our products. Our dolls were too delicate and expensive for children because they were never intended for them. Our doll collectors were women in their thirties and forties, many of whom had been too poor in their childhoods to be able to play with fancy dolls. In effect, they had been waiting years to hold their Scarletts. We were meeting a demand that had been pent up for decades.

Similarly, we created die-cast cars for male collectors. These were the cars of their youth, the cars they would have proudly taken out on the boulevard on Saturday night and to the drive-in on Sunday—if only they'd had the money. Given the powerful emotions they evoked, it was all the more important that these products delivered quality and value. When you buy a cheap piece of junk and it breaks down, you get angry at yourself for being so stupid. But when you buy an expensive product that touches you emotionally and that product fails you, you experience that disappointment as betrayal. In addition to feeling used and hurt, you get angry. Our collectibles had to deliver both emotional satisfaction and high quality.

Our success depended on keen consumer insight. We conducted research and focus groups to understand our collectors' deepest motivations and desires. Then we set out to meet their highest hopes. I've always believed in giving people more than they expect. It compliments not only their taste but their awareness and intelligence.

> Give people more than they expect—it compliments their taste and their intelligence.

We staffed a research library that housed the artistic history of civilization. Through the efforts of our earnest librarians we could ensure that every detail of our products was authentic and true. I brought in decorative art scholars to educate the staff on everything from Gothic Revival and American Federal to French Rococo. When we copied a style, I wanted it to be accurate in every way. I hired prominent artists to sculpt the faces of our dolls. Their miniature clothes were meticulously tailored—right down to the fabric, the buttons, even the lace. Most of the dolls retailed for about $200, but some went as high as $500 and a few for more than $1,000.

Similarly, our cars were hand-assembled, die-cast, and built exactly—and I mean *exactly*—to scale with as many as 130 parts. They had baked-on enamel and doors that swung open, hoods that lifted, and steering wheels that turned. If the original automobile had leather seats, our model had leather seats. If it had spoke wheels, our model had spoke wheels. We sold them for as much as $145, but that was a small price to pay to own the car of your dreams. It wasn't long before one program, Cars of the Fifties, accounted for the biggest business the Franklin Mint had ever done, more than $125 million in sales.

To me, the Mint was all about the rubies. Precision, craftsmanship, and careful attention to detail were essential—and we were able to charge a very healthy markup for delivering them. Because we cared about the intrinsic value of everything we produced, we attracted a loyal base of collectors who knew they got their money's worth when they purchased from us. We understood that our products had emotional resonance. If you've always wanted a Rolls-

Royce Silver Shadow but could never afford one, that die-cast model is a lot more than just a shiny toy.

We had offices around the world and our staff and labor force was so large—it peaked at around 4,500—that we had huge expenses and overhead. But our profits justified the expense. In our first seven years, we took the business from $150 million a year in sales to nearly $1 billion. Given the volume of the Mint, it made sense to begin sourcing in Malaysia and China. We built our own factories, installed air-conditioning, and provided health care and hot meals to employees.

In order to keep the pipeline stocked with new products, I had a concept group whose sole task was to develop ideas: high-end dolls, collector plates, die-cast cars, male and female jewelry, bronzes, sculpture, porcelain figurines, coins, religious icons, doll houses, home decor, and on and on. We tested anywhere from 1,000 to 1,500 new product ideas a year. We gauged how in tune we were with the market by the percentage of ideas that stuck.

Our business was global. We had separate product lines for the United Kingdom, Germany, France, and Japan. Fifteen and twenty years ago, the world was less homogeneous, and individual markets were more distinct. Each had its own tastes.

Our licensing group was dedicated to acquiring the rights to old movies, beloved brands of bygone eras, plus stars such as Elvis Presley, Elizabeth Taylor, and John Wayne. We secured the rights to Marilyn Monroe directly from the estate of her acting teacher, Lee Strasberg. By the time I was finished teaching myself about her short, tumultuous life, I could tell you practically every line she had ever uttered in a movie and describe just about every costume she had ever worn.

To introduce our Marilyn doll collection (with Marilyn in the pink bow gown, of course), I needed a fine artist who could capture Marilyn's unique mixture of innocence and raw sex appeal. I chose Emily Kaufman, but unfortunately, she demurred. Eventually, I convinced her that when she created a singular work of art, only one person could own it. But if she created a Marilyn sculpture for the Franklin Mint, thousands of people could own, enjoy, and treasure her work.

Emily went on to create the entire line of Marilyn dolls for the Mint. Of course, there have been thousands of representations of Marilyn across every imaginable medium, but I don't think anyone ever captured the essence of Marilyn Monroe in quite the "art imitates life" way Emily did for the Franklin Mint.

Our licensing operation extended well beyond celebrities. In addition, we licensed Harley-Davidson along with practically every car company in the world, the Victoria and Albert Museum, the Louvre, and even the Vatican— in the first-ever licensing deal of its kind. We located an original member of the Fabergé family and licensed the name of the famous creators of Fabergé eggs. We were able to reproduce priceless museum pieces that you didn't have to be a tsar to collect.

All of our designs and illustrations were done in-house,

as was the advertising, which emphasized both the history behind a product and the Mint's fine attention to detail. In all our communications, we delivered the same message to collectors over and over again: We care.

Having earned our collectors' faith, we were able to take what might otherwise have seemed outrageous gambles—by spending millions on new product development. We licensed the right to produce our own Monopoly game. I figured that when you play Monopoly, you're playing at being a real estate mogul, buying and selling property. You're just like Donald Trump, right? So what kind of board would Donald Trump play on? A gorgeous, natural mahogany board with gold hotels and silver houses, that's what. That's the Monopoly board we designed and sold—at $550. The set grossed more than $150 million in revenue during its lifetime.

We did a great business in Japan when its economy was booming. We sold sake sets, scrolls, representations of Mount Fuji, coins, dolls, and much, much more. When the Japanese economy practically ground to a halt in the early 1990s, we shifted gears and did just as well.

I was a close student of Japanese culture and economics. I knew the good times were coming to an end; jobs would be tight, and expense accounts would all but disappear. Japanese men, who were used to going out every night after work, would be spending nights at home for the first time since the samurai returned from battle. So I bought the Japanese rights to Time-Life videos and did a great business in war documentaries, wild animal programs, and other videos targeted at these newly domesticated men.

If there is one venture that captured the essence of what was best about our business at the Mint, I think it would have to be the story of Jackie Kennedy's pearls. Nothing I've ever done is more illustrative of the search for intrinsic value than that. Nothing better captures the effort to locate the rubies in the orchard.

You know the pearls I'm talking about. Jacqueline Kennedy was so often photographed wearing those pearls that they seemed a natural extension of her—an integral piece of her legendary grace and charm. She wore them to state dinners. She wore them on trips to India, Greece, and Japan. She wore them when she greeted the high and mighty and when she was looking after the children. Believe me—you *know* those pearls! But what you may not know is that the pearls were fake. Jacqueline Bouvier purchased them at Bergdorf Goodman in the 1950s for about $35.00.

I worshiped Jackie Kennedy all my life. To me, she was the epitome of class; she managed to be beautiful and refined while still being refreshing, rather than stodgy or uptight. And I was certainly not alone in my admiration. For millions of American women, Jackie was the standard by which every woman on the public stage was judged. She was the closest we would have to American royalty.

In 1996, Sotheby's announced its "Auction of the Century" to sell the estate of Jacqueline Kennedy Onassis. I attacked the auction catalogs like a rabid librarian who had just been released from the gulag. Yet despite my affection for the subject and my appreciation of her belongings, I could find only one thing in the entire auction that I wanted: those pearls. My staff was shocked by my restraint.

The catalog listed the estimate on the pearls at $200 to $300. Shrewd as I was, I suspected they might go a bit higher. In the weeks before the auction, I realized—time and time again—what a truly naive notion that was. As I kept pace with the constantly revised estimate on the pearls, I did my best to keep Stewart up to date.

"Darling, I think we may have to go as high as five thousand dollars to get those pearls," I told him.

"They're fake, right?" he asked. "That's insane."

As the auction day neared, I gave Stewart the latest. "I think Jackie's pearls may go as high as twenty-five thousand dollars," I said.

"For a set of fake pearls? That's just nuts."

By this point, I had already talked myself into buying them. I wanted to convince Stewart that the investment—as crazy as it seemed—would be worthwhile. I spread photos across Stewart's desk—Jackie in the pearls here, Jackie in the pearls there, John-John on Jackie's lap pulling at those same pearls.

"She wore them in nearly every picture ever taken," I said. "They are the icon of the icon."

The day before the auction, the estimates were truly, undeniably insane—off the charts. I told Stewart the pearls might go for a ridiculous amount—maybe even $100,000.

He just stared with incomprehension. The next day, big, brave me handed the phone to Stewart. I knew he had the guts to go all the way, provided I had actually convinced him. I guess I had. The starting price was $5,000. By the time the hammer came down on our winning bid, we had agreed to a final price of $211,000. We now owned the most expensive strand of fake pearls in the entire world.

We were not the only ones astonished by our willingness to pay such an absurd price. *People* magazine ran a story on the pearls, as did most U.S. newspapers. Dewar's Scotch took out a full-page ad in *The Wall Street Journal* with the headline "Just pay $211,000.00 for a strand of fake pearls? You need a Dewar's."

We sent two guards from the Mint's private army (we stored large supplies of gold and silver because of our on-site minting operation) to New York to bring back the pearls. They delivered them to me directly at work. Everyone stood around and watched the unveiling. The pearls were still in their original silk-lined box from Bergdorf's. As I opened it, I caught a faint scent of Jackie's perfume. It was a chilling experience. My eyes welled up as I thought about what that divine creature had meant to me and my country.

We analyzed the 139 European glass faux pearls and made exact reproductions from a mold. The pearls were color-matched to the creamy originals, with the same seventeen coats of lacquer that the originals possessed. Then they were put on hand-knotted silken cords. The circle was closed by a silver art deco clasp featuring nine period-style rhinestones and bearing a Franklin Mint silver monogrammed emblem of authenticity. They were as close to the real fake Jackie pearls that any combination of art and technology could muster.

We put the original strand of pearls on a coast-to-coast tour before bringing them home and exhibiting them at the Franklin Mint Museum. A couple of years ago, we made a gift of them to the nation; they are permanently on view at the Smithsonian.

At $211,000, the pearls turned out to be a phenomenal bargain. We sold more than 130,000 copies at $200 a strand—for a gross of $26 million. Owning the original pearls gave us the credibility to sell the copies; it certified and rewarded our collectors' faith that they were getting as close to the real deal as anyone could. By wearing those iconic pearls, women everywhere could channel a bit of Jackie.

It mattered that we studied and analyzed the pearls. It mattered that our reproductions were made from exact molds of the originals. It mattered that we replicated the color, the cord, and every detail as faithfully as science would allow. In the end, it mattered that we cared about the pearls every bit as much as our collectors cared. That bond—that faith in the product and what it represented—is ultimately what transformed 139 spheres of ordinary glass into genuine rubies—with real and lasting intrinsic value.

Value is real, even when the product is 100 percent fake.

We included a Letter of Authenticity in every shipment of every product we created and marketed. It was more than a letter; it was a creed. Our dolls weren't just pretty ladies in frilly dresses, plucked randomly from some designer's fantasy. They had history and character. Our cars were painstakingly exact. And if we did our homework right, our collectors would see that we had been true to the history and character of the original—down to the smallest detail. It was Mies van der Rohe who said, "God is in the details." So is value. So is faith. Hey, so is life.

CHAPTER 5

Thinking Inside the Pomegranate

I n the early 1970s, General Foods, which was happily selling its Kool-Aid brand sugar powder by the ton, looked around for a way to sell a similar concoction that adults wouldn't be ashamed to drink. The company developed a lemon-flavored powder and conducted extensive research to determine how best to market it. They came up with the folksy name Country Time and sold it with the promise that, even though it was sold in canisters at the supermarket, once this powder was mixed with water it tasted just like "good, old-fashioned lemonade."

The product was hawked on TV by a "white-haired grandfather, suspenders and all, sitting on a sun-drenched porch on a sizzling summer day mixing up a pitcher of ice-cold lemonade."[1] Who could resist? It wasn't long before

---

[1]Allen P. Adamson, *BrandSimple.*

Country Time was selling big and Grandpa was snapping his suspenders to the tune of "I'm in the money."

At least until the day Minute Maid ran a negative ad that exposed Country Time for what it was: a fraud. As it happened, not a single lemon went into the creation of that "good, old-fashioned lemonade." Not one. The Minute Maid ad killed Country Time and took the whole powdered lemonade category down with it.

So what do you know?! It turns out people don't like being lied to and having their trust betrayed. It cost Minute Maid a pretty penny in advertising to make this point in the 1970s. Today, they could put up a virtually cost-free but no less devastating ad on YouTube, sit back, and enjoy the viral destruction of a competitor in a millisecond.

To me, the Country Time fiasco is the essence of "thinking outside the box." For years, we've been told that society's smartest, most creative, and biggest winners all think that way, and if we don't, we must be missing that special edge required for success. At management conferences and sales retreats, in business books and corporate seminars, we are exhorted by some guru or another to leave our foolish boxes behind.

Bear with me a moment as I pose a somewhat obvious question. How many successful people have you met in your entire life who can really, truly "think outside the box"? When was the last time you encountered someone who is able to conceptualize and create something that is truly new—something unlike anything that has come before?

Einstein could do that. For a contemporary business

example, I guess you could say Steve Jobs has done it, as did the brilliant technologists who devised the Internet. I've been privileged to meet some of the best business minds in the world, but I can count on one hand—maybe two—the number of people who really, truly "think outside the box."

One of them is my friend Michael Milken, who made a fortune with his invention of high-yield bonds. Mike has similarly built his Milken Family Foundation into an innovative force for good. Since 1982, he has invested in educational opportunity and saved hundreds of thousands of lives by directing medical research and health care outreach in pursuit of faster cures, particularly of prostate cancer.

Creative geniuses like Mike don't need business schools to inspire their ideas because they already view the world in a multidimensional context; it's a picture the rest of us, with our linear lines of sight, can't fully grasp. The vast majority of people, including those who are most successful in business, think inside the box.

This is not an incidental point, because it's easy to be awed by someone who comes up with a product or solution that you presume you never would have thought of yourself. It's easy to attribute their insight to a flash of genius that you don't share or to special talents you can't emulate. It's easy to assume that they achieve their success by thinking outside that box in which the rest of us spend our working hours. These flashes of genius, the subject of Malcolm Gladwell's *Blink: The Power of Thinking Without Thinking*, may seem to emerge out of the thinnest air.

More often, they are the product of years of experience and accumulated knowledge.

Art historian E. H. Gombrich said, "There's no such thing as the immaculate perception." He was right. New perceptions, just like new creations, are inevitably cobbled together from what has been experienced, perceived, or created before. Just as the first typewriter was derived from the telegraph transmitter and the first motorcycle from the bicycle, most breakthroughs are grounded in knowledge and experience. They don't descend from the ether. Every so often, an inventor takes a concept from one realm and applies it ingeniously to another. Reebok, for example, got the idea for its Pump sneaker from the inflatable insert used in a hospital IV bag.

Most of us are products of a society, culture, and educational system that have enormous influence in structuring the way we think. For every great idea that is generated outside those confines, there are thousands more that are the product of thinking inside the box—by people who have been working at solving a problem for a long time. As Thomas Edison said, "Genius is one percent inspiration and ninety-nine percent perspiration."

What we nongeniuses are apt to achieve when we think outside the box is something unhinged from reality, like good old-fashioned lemonade made without a single lemon. This is especially tempting to marketers trying to sell a brand that has no intrinsic value—in which case, reality doesn't give you a whole lot to work with.

Stewart and I have designed all of our companies to facilitate and encourage thinking inside the box, to allow us to go deeper and deeper into our brands to find more value there. The most obvious example of that is our preference for in-house work over outside consultants. I mentioned before that Bryan Honkawa developed our distinctive POM bottle. Bryan is our top in-house designer, but he is far more than that; he is a marketer, too. He and I have worked together for more than twenty years; he is there when ideas are born, and he attends most of the meetings where brands are created and developed. He knows his stuff—but he also knows our stuff. So when he creates a product, it is grounded in the brand and in all the knowledge of the brand that comes from being part of the team.

All of our advertising, media buying, public relations, and product design are created in-house, as well. Why? Well, one of the reasons I got out of advertising in the first place is that I started to feel that my efforts were mostly window dressing. My experiences with outside consultants have convinced me that, most of the time, their solutions tend to be both quick and shallow. That doesn't mean that from time to time I don't allow hope to triumph over experience, much like a second marriage. But I realize that consultants, too, are in business. Their mission is to maximize profit from the work they do—to get it in, get it done, and get it out in record time. That is how they are judged by their bosses. I'm not saying there isn't great talent out there; I just want that talent to work *with* us, as part of our team, rather than *for* us, as a consultant who has more than one client and agenda.

There are times, however, when we are faced with a

special project so big or so urgent or so far outside our comfort zone that we must rely on outside talent. In those instances, we *manage* the heck out of the process—even at the risk of becoming the clients from Hell. One thing we never do is leave our brand at the mercy of chance.

When I hire people full-time from the agency world, we reindoctrinate them and teach them our ways. I want creative solutions with no borrowed interest. The mission is straightforward: Get to know the brand you are working on, live with it day in and day out. Then create break-through advertising and programs born from the Unique Selling Proposition of the brand. At our companies, that is how we solve problems—and break new ground.

The one constant, whether the work comes from our own team or from guns for hire, is that the product is only as good as the brief that goes into it. I always say I want a marketing brief so tight that if the author were run over by a bus, anyone could pick up the project and complete it.

We take the same in-house approach to management consulting. Rather than hire McKinsey or Bain to help us sort through new ideas, potential acquisitions, and deals, we have created our own McKinsey in-house. Roll International, which is the umbrella company for all of our businesses, employs about twenty top-notch MBAs as a full-time, in-house consulting force. And just like our creative staff, our consultants become invested in the success of some part of our business and bring all of their talent and intelligence to bear on it. For example, they have been integral to helping us master the challenges of growth at POM, analyzing our operations and helping us design processes for juicing and bottling that maximize efficiency and minimize waste.

In any business, there are inevitably projects that deserve more attention than they receive. A project that's potentially crucial to long-term growth may not seem sufficiently urgent to capture the attention of managers immersed in day-to-day operations. Like many executives, our managers are often too busy to perform due diligence on every opportunity for new business creation or for the extension of an existing business. That's when our consulting team steps in. Since our in-house consultants are already part of our extended family, their advice is always valued. Just as important, we are able to evaluate it without fearing it stems from an ulterior business motive. Sadly, not everyone who hires an outside consulting firm can be so confident.

Our consulting team is also a phenomenal talent pool for management. POM president Matt Tupper came out of our consulting team, as did the presidents of FIJI Water and Teleflora. We had worked with them for a few years before they took over management responsibilities. We knew exactly what we were getting into—and so did they.

Another benefit we get from our in-house focus is hard to measure, but it's vitally important. We have a coherent business culture. Everyone is pulling in the same direction. Everyone understands our philosophy of searching for rubies in the orchard, digging deep to find value, and being truthful in communicating that value to consum-

ers. We don't get a lot of people engaging in shady behavior—although when we've encountered this, it's almost
always been instigated by an employee who joined us from
a public company. In other words, someone who was accustomed to answering Wall Street's call of the wild.

At one of our companies, we hired a young fellow
straight out of an investment banking firm to be our chief
financial officer. He had a habit of making the financials
look rosier than they actually were. We kept explaining to
him that our company is privately held, that we needed to
see a true picture in order to run our business, but the poor
chap was so accustomed to manufacturing crooked numbers each quarter for "The Street" that he couldn't find his
way back to the straight and narrow. If he had exhibited a
drinking or substance abuse problem, we could have sent
him to rehab, but where do you send a recidivist hooked
on funny financials? We had to let him go.

You can't cook value any more than you can cook
books. Sooner or later, it's bound to stink up the kitchen.
POM's success is purely a consequence of avoiding the
extrinsic and extraneous and instead going deeper inside
the pomegranate, where the value resides.

We got into the pomegranate business with a helpful
push from happenstance. In 1986, Stewart bought a large
pistachio orchard and discovered that the sale included
more than 100 acres of pomegranates. "Let's pull them
and plant more nuts," one of Stewart's farmers advised.
Stewart is successful not only because he's smart. He's successful in part because he keeps himself open to new op-

Until the launch of POM Wonderful in 2002, pomegranates were virtually unknown by American consumers.

"Cut through the clutter" billboard advertising has proved successful for the entire line of POM products.

teleflora

*Teleflora's Flowers-in-a-Gift was the
Unique Selling Proposition that
revolutionized the industry (and
earned a Gold Effie for marketing).*

We bought Jackie Kennedy's fake pearls at auction for the outlandish sum of $211,000. We sold 130,000 copies for $200 a strand.

THE FRANKLIN MINT

The Franklin Mint developed a wide variety of collectibles to appeal to more than 8 million collectors worldwide.

fijigreen.com

From the islands of

FIJI®

NATURAL ARTESIAN WATER

**Carbon negative.
Globally positive.**

At FIJI Water our mission has always been to bring you the finest, best-tasting water on earth. To ensure this for years to come, we're going "carbon negative." Which means reducing CO_2 emissions across all of our products. Changing 50% of our bottling facility's energy to renewable sources by 2010. And partnering with Conservation International to help save the largest rainforest in Fiji. Making FIJI Water the first carbon-negative product in our industry. And perhaps the most positive for the world.

fijigreen.com

*FIJI is the first bottled water, and maybe the first
food product in America, to become carbon negative.*

portunities. And he knows how to be patient. "Let's see how they do," he replied. Those five little words would create an industry.

Stewart soon learned that when the pomegranates did well, they could earn a better return than pistachios. He planted another 6,000 acres over the next decade. As pomegranates became a more significant business for us, we set out to learn more about them. That's when we began to discover the folklore and references in ancient texts about the fruit's remarkable healing powers.

In 1996, we began subjecting the health properties of the pomegranate to the proving ground of modern medicine. Stewart and our medical adviser, Dr. Leslie Dornfeld, met with Dr. Michael Aviram, an Israeli scientist who had done seminal research into the antioxidant powers of red wine. Stewart and Dr. Dornfeld asked him to begin research on the pomegranate, as well.

Antioxidants have increasingly been the subject of

POM Wonderful Antioxidant Potency Index.

medical research because they are capable of neutralizing free radicals, the unstable molecules that appear to damage cells and tissue and may be linked to disease and aging. Research by Dr. Aviram and others revealed that POM has 17 percent more polyphenol antioxidants than red wine and neutralizes 54 percent more free radicals. Prior to this discovery, red wine had been the antioxidant king, so the research findings were cause for a toast.

We went on to fund independent studies assessing the effects of pomegranate juice on cardiovascular disease, cancer—especially prostate cancer—and type 2 diabetes. Across the board, the findings ranged from propitious to downright startling. For example, a UCLA study revealed a significantly slower PSA doubling time for men who drank eight ounces of POM daily after having been treated for prostate cancer. (A slower doubling time may reflect slower progression of the disease.)

This research was costly; so far, we've spent nearly $25 million to explore the health benefits of POM, but it's been worth every penny because we now understand the value of these rubies in the orchard—and their enormous potential for good.

The pomegranate is a beautiful fruit, but there is also something a little weird about it. You can look up and down the fresh food aisle at the market and you won't encounter anything quite like it. That's because the pomegranate occupies its own branch on the evolutionary tree; it's an outlier with no direct relatives in the plant world, a Galápagos unto itself.

Having evolved in the highlands of Central Asia, the pomegranate found a cherished place in the packs of travelers and in the holds of ships. Over the course of months, while a pomegranate turns a dark, baked-brown color outside, the inside remains packed with sugar and other nutrients. In fact, its peel provides such an impervious coat of armor that the fruit can remain juicy for months after it has been picked.

So far, the research we've funded has yielded about two dozen published reports, which are available on the pom wonderful.com Web site. We have about thirty more studies in the works. Since the scientific standards on health claims are high, however, even some of the most promising research goes largely unheralded in our marketing.

Scientific data is not the only measure of POM's success, of course. Lots of people drink POM because it makes them *feel* healthier—data or no data—and that feeling has been a significant driver of our growth. Our fresh pomegranate sales went from 100,000 cartons in 2001 to 1.9 million cartons in 2007. Similarly, in just four years, POM has gone from zero to $165 million in sales—with an advertising budget that is a tiny fraction of what you would expect to launch a new product in the packaged goods industry.

Over the years, we've continued planting more acreage, growing more fruit, and building the market for both fresh pomegranates and our juice. Today we have more than 18,000 acres planted with pomegranates, and we keep expanding our orchards.

However, as we built up our juicing operations and our juice market, we faced two issues. Some POM drinkers were looking for a lighter drink that would still deliver the antioxidant power of POM. In fact, lots of POM drinkers had developed ritualistic ways of diluting POM, mixing it with seltzer or tea or lemonade or any number of other combinations to make it less like a weighty Burgundy and more like a light thirst quencher. Meanwhile, diabetics were eager to have a version of POM with less sugar.

It made sense for us to respond to this demand and offer consumers a light POM. That may sound easy, but when you're dealing with the world's most oddball fruit, things are seldom easy. If you dilute the unique sugars and phytochemicals in pomegranate juice—nutrients that occur nowhere else in nature—you undermine its anti-oxidant properties. Making a light version of POM simply wasn't possible without making the kind of compromises we are unwilling to make.

At the same time that we faced this quandary over light juice, we were trying to figure out what to do with tens of thousands of tons of discarded, mashed-up pome-granates left over from the juicing process. The pungent discards also possessed incredible nutritional value; the fruit's highest concentration of antioxidants is found in the peel, which has unique and powerful tannins. And the arils inside the pomegranate contain rare oil, stocked with unique compounds.

We had been selling this mash as cattle feed, all the time thinking "Wouldn't it be great if we could find some way to salvage the extraordinary health properties contained in this mound of reddish ooze?" I'm all for a happy Elsie but I would rather bring the powerful potion to people. The ideal would be a product more scalable than juice, something we could send around the world to meet the demand for health, but in a different way.

This innocent notion led to much consternation at POM. My marketing team and I were eager to learn if we could produce a pomegranate extract that could deliver the power of eight ounces of POM juice in a capsule. The operations team howled. We were asking too much. They had already performed a series of miracles to produce POM. Remember, pomegranates are as fickle as Goldilocks; as I explained in chapter 1, squeeze them too hard, and they produce bitter juice; squeeze them too little, and they will deny you both profit and health benefits. What's more, production of a pomegranate extract would necessitate a whole new round of science to determine whether it was safe and effective.

I've never been one to give up easily (or otherwise), so you may have guessed the outcome: Marketing won over Operations. We went to work developing a pomegranate extract. After a couple years of testing, we came up with an ultrapotent, 100 percent pure polyphenol antioxidant extract made from the same California pomegranates we use to make POM. We called it POMx. The mound of red ooze had delivered big time. But we still had one more hurdle.

The supplement market is a con man's Shangri-La,

crowded with dubious products hawked by fly-by-night marketers hailing from the sleazier precincts of the business world. Though virtually tone deaf, I feel more confident betting on the winner of *American Idol* than on the efficacy of a container of capsules at the local "nutrition" store. After years of investment, hard work, and testing—including the only safety review of a pomegranate supplement conducted by the Food and Drug Administration—I wasn't eager for POMx to keep company with the supplement crowd.

What to do? Distribution is everything in a new-product introduction. As brilliant, portable, shelf-stable, and pure as this supplement is, finding its market is our greatest challenge. In fact, putting the equivalent of eight ounces of juice into one little pill is nothing compared to finding the right direct-marketing campaign. At this writing, we are in a test phase, selling the pills online through the POM Web site and a dedicated site, PomPills.com. We are testing print ads in health, fitness, and general-interest magazines, and in media with broader reach, and we also have an online campaign.

> Distribution is everything in a new product introduction.

Yet we also realized that POMx is a fabulous ingredient that could enhance a wide range of products. While we were developing POMx, we were also thinking about how we might produce a tea that would meet the high standards established by POM. The tea seemed like a great idea, but it lacked the antioxidant punch that is integral to the POM brand. So we put the idea on a shelf, where it stayed for about a year.

POMx brought it back. With POMx in the mix, we could produce a tea replete with the remarkable antioxidant properties our consumers craved. We used hand-picked tea leaves and a brewing process not unlike that for sun tea. One result of our exceptionally gentle extraction process is a taste that's both delicate and delicious. Another result is that every flavor in the line has less than four milligrams of caffeine—an infant can drink it. With its lighter taste, fewer calories, and all-natural ingredients, POM Tea was the product we'd been searching for. After bottling our new brew inside a beautifully rendered keepsake glass, we went to market.

I don't want to give the impression that all this magically came together. It didn't. In fact, it was a struggle every step of the way. One problem with our tea was price; POMx is expensive to process in a form that lends itself to mixing with other liquids. In addition, most ready-to-drink teas on the market are made with powdered teas or low-end product. I wanted handpicked tea leaves brewed in a way that wouldn't cause the bitterness associated with other teas. I also refused to use high-fructose corn syrup, which is much cheaper than natural sugars.

Each time I put my foot down in the name of quality, the price soared. Then I made the problem worse by insisting on creating a keepsake glass. We didn't intend to use it forever, because eventually plastic is the way to go for both consumers and the environment. But I was searching for a way for POM Tea to stand out on the shelf while the brand was introduced. I wanted my consumer to know immediately that this wasn't your grandma's Snapple.

The money and time invested in POMx and POM Tea were money and time denied to other potential breakthroughs, and there was no guarantee of success. The path we followed was charted by our faith in our product and confidence that we could convince the marketplace to share our faith. In the end, POM Tea costs twice as much as—or more than—most of the competition, so we needed faith not only in the value of our product but in our ability to communicate that value and in consumers' ability to recognize it and embrace it. The success of POM Tea proved that our brand had enough equity and elasticity that we could afford to venture into new terrain.

I had always wanted to create a healthy energy drink. I was kept up at night fretting that half our hyperdriven society was imbibing the likes of bulls' adrenal glands in search of a liquid energy boost. Ugh. The ingredients in most energy drinks are more likely to be found in a chemistry lab than a farmer's market—this stuff isn't Popeye's spinach. I thought if we could come up with a natural energy drink packed with the antioxidant power of POMx, we would have another winner. We worked on it for several years, frequently banging our heads against the wall before shelving the idea. But of course, through near successes and total failures, we also learned a lot.

One of the things we learned was that POMx seemed to taste especially good with dairy products. In fact, Stewart had acquired a habit of mixing POMx in yogurt smoothies. So we decided to give it a try with coffee and milk.

One of the funny things about developing new food products is that you always know when you have a hit—and when you don't. If, after the presentation has been made, everyone gets up from the conference table and files out, leaving the test product in a half-consumed state on the table, you know you need to go back to the drawing board. If, on the other hand, the presentation ends and people seem to be lingering a little too long, availing themselves of another taste and eyeing the dregs in the containers, you know you've just passed the test.

Our chief food scientist had been experimenting with POMx and coffee. Among the few of us who had tasted this mixture, the enthusiasm—it was more like love—was overflowing. We needed a reality check. So we had a POM Coffee tasting at our house. When it was all over, we found people sneaking around our kitchen scrounging for leftovers. Something about this delicious combination of coffee and POMx just does that to people. As I write this, we're launching four flavors of POMx Coffee: chocolate, café au lait, caramel, and chai tea (yes, I know chai is not coffee, but it was so good we couldn't bear to leave it out of the lineup). We use ethically sourced, Rainforest Alliance Certified, premium Italian-roasted Arabica coffee beans, organic sugar, and milk from cows that aren't doped up with artificial hormones. And this drink really packs a wallop; a ten-ounce bottle has all the antioxidants, courtesy of POMx, of an eight-ounce glass of POM Juice.

Like all faith, brand faith is tested from time to time. In

2006, right when POM was really taking off as a brand, we faced a crisis. Demand had grown threefold in the prior two years. Supply had not. In fact, our crop yield that year was a major disappointment. That's one thing about agriculture—you can't simply keep the factory open round the clock to increase supply. Nature doesn't do business that way.

So at the moment when we should have been basking in our success, enjoying the huge spike in demand for our product, we were in a state of panic. Our stores were running out of POM, and we had none on hand to supply them. Our customers, big supermarkets and other retail establishments that we had worked very hard to cultivate, were extremely unhappy with us. Worse, our consumers, some of whom had grown accustomed to drinking POM every day, were traveling from store to store in a literally fruitless search for our juice. They wanted their POM fix, and they wanted it *now*.

We tried to explain. We hadn't expected so much success. There had been too much sun that year. The rains had come late. The bees hadn't been in the mood. All of these explanations were true, but to healthy juice addicts looking for their fix, frantically searching store shelves for an ever-dwindling supply, the truth was not very comforting.

As we scrambled to find some way to meet demand and keep our customers and consumers from deserting us, suddenly, on the horizon, it looked like our ship was coming in. Agents approached us with an offer of an enormous tanker full of Iranian pomegranate juice. It seemed like a godsend. After all, these agents were not the only ones who had noticed the huge, unmet demand for pomegranate juice. Everyone from small juice makers right up to Pepsi-Cola suddenly sensed a great opportunity to make inroads in a growing new market—at our expense. If we didn't buy the Iranian juice, someone else surely would—and they would use it to try to lure away our retail customers and consumers.

We were running so low on juice that we were cutting retail orders by 60 percent or more. As we debated what to do, we realized we really had no choice. The only responsible decision we could make was to resign ourselves to fate. We grow the Wonderful variety of pomegranates, and we grow them in our own way, on our own land, in our home state of California. My husband the farmer and his able staff run the best orchards in the world, where the science of modern agriculture meets the culture of old-world farming. The juicing plant is state of the art, our presses are so unique that they are a carefully protected trade secret, and we transport our product in refrigerated trucks to keep the juice fresh.

Let's assume, for the purposes of debate, that the Iranian shipment was truly 100 percent pomegranate juice. How did the farmers care for their fields? What kind of fertilizer or pesticides might they have used? How did they harvest the crop? How did they squeeze the pomegranates? We didn't know the answer to any of these questions, and we knew we wouldn't really be able to verify any of the answers we were given.

So how could we make the same claims about this Iranian juice—healthwise, tastewise, qualitywise—that we made about POM? The only way we could be sure would be to test the efficacy of the Iranian juice against POM's. That would take months, even years. Meantime, with all those question marks hanging in the air, if there was even one ounce of the Iranian juice in a POM bottle, it simply wasn't right to call it POM.

After analyzing the possibilities from every angle—believe me, we really wanted to meet the demand and make everyone happy—we circled back to where the company had started. Corporate mission statements can be awful things—full of false piety, hypocrisy, nonsense, garbled, strained language, and outright falsehoods. The worst of them are enough to make your skin crawl. When we formulated a mission statement for POM a few years before, we meant what we said:

> *Unique as the pomegranate itself—tough and protective on the outside, mythically beautiful on the inside—POM Wonderful is a global brand committed to creating an entrepreneurial legacy of innovation, profitability and wellness, by growing and marketing the highest quality pomegranates and pomegranate-based products that are healthy, honest and essential to the well-being of humankind.*

We knew that our own pomegranates and pomegranate-based products were of the highest quality; they were healthy, honest, and essential to the well-being of human-kind. They passed the test. We didn't know if the Iranian juice had been produced in a test tube on the dark side of the moon. If we meant what we said, we had no choice but to leave the Iranian stuff at sea, where it soon found another buyer.

The decision hurt us. In addition to losing money, we spent more time placating our retailers and answering customer service calls than we did running our business. But, as often happens when you opt to do the right thing, in the long run, it was probably good for business. It underscored our brand's integrity and the promise of freshness and quality, and it's certainly not the worst thing to have consumers angry and upset and yelling at the supermarket manager because they're craving your product and can't find it. Better that than a shrug of the shoulders! We posted an apology on our Web site, explaining that we simply didn't have enough supply to meet demand, and from grocery shelves that had formerly stocked POM, we dangled cards with the message: "Out of juice? So are we."

> As often happens when you opt to do the right thing, in the long run it is probably good for business.

The pomegranate shortage was a real threat to our business. Yet inside every threat is an opportunity. In fact, a great business consultant named Ichak Adizes, whom we worked with in the late 1980s, used to call these pivotal moments "oppor-threats," because like yin and yang, they always come in pairs. In this instance, the shortage prompted us to start thinking seriously about developing line extensions that would be less dependent on Mother Nature and the idiosyncrasies of our unique fruit. POMx and POM Tea were both products of crisis that catalyzed general talk into specific action. The way a business (or nation) handles oppor-threats goes a long way in determining its success or failure. For POM, the danger passed and the opportunity expanded.

> Inside every threat is an opportunity.

The following year, our pomegranates came back strong with a bumper crop—a karma crop. This little parable of the juices has a lot to do with business honesty. It has a lot to do with understanding the upside of an oppor-threat. It also has to do with intrinsic value. We spent a lot of time and invested a lot of creative energy in devising the right name, packaging, and design for our brand. If we had believed that our iconic bottle or some other extrinsic element was the source of value, we could have put any old juice inside and called it POM, but we didn't—because we staked our value on the real thing inside, the juice.

We were able to recover from a shortage of POM on supermarket shelves. It's doubtful we could have recovered from betraying our own claims and the trust of our consumers. Does anyone believe a word that any cigarette maker has said in recent decades—about *anything?* Will parents simply forgive and forget that Mattel sold them tainted toys for their children to play with? I doubt it.

When prospective partners have proposed POM brand extensions, we've tried to keep in mind our mission and our understanding of value. Once you become successful, you have to be disciplined enough—and care deeply enough about your product—to leave money on the table from time to time. We've had offers to put POM in everything from candy to shampoo. But we're very protective of our brand equity. Any deal that might trivialize or dilute that equity is not in POM's long-term interest, regardless of how much revenue it might generate in the short term.

> In building a successful business, you have to be disciplined enough to leave money on the table.

Value and values have a similar root: authenticity. And when you damage one side of the equation, the other side just doesn't add up. Consider the example of a famous pizza chain. Instead of focusing on a value proposition—a modest pizza at an inexpensive price—Domino's hired the blond bombshell Jessica Simpson for its advertising campaign. The ads were served up extra hot, with Jessica's bodacious bod as the appetizer, main course, and dessert. A short time later, however, the pizza girl let it slip that she is allergic to wheat, tomatoes, and cheese, which is another way of saying she can't stand pizza. Domino's ended up looking like a fraud—and not a very clever one at that. How did a large, successful company get itself into such a mess? I think I know. Someone in marketing at Domino's was thinking outside the pizza box.

CHAPTER 6

Thinking Inside the Volcano

I t was a sunny summer day in Aspen. Stewart and I were on one of our Bataan Death Marches over the mountains. "We've been approached by a water company that's for sale," Stewart told me. I should have known by now how to detect another big job lurking behind his nonchalance, but my thirst for a challenge distracted me.

"Water?" I gasped. His timing was impeccable. My own water bottle was running low, and I was thirsty. "That's a really crowded category," I panted through parched lips, "and they all taste the same anyway." As it happened, I would later eat—or drink—those words.

To say the bottled water market is "crowded" doesn't really do justice to the colossal clutter of it all. There are more than six hundred brands of bottled water flooding the United States. There is filtered tap water gushing from that giant spigot known as Coca-Cola, which has a distribution network extending to every giant supermarket and corner bodega in the nation. There are countless local springs and wells—the water from which finds its way into regional bottled waters such as Adirondack in upstate New York and Calistoga in California. There are stylish European waters such as Voss and Acqua Panna. And there are hundreds of others that fall into one of those categories—or somewhere in between. Why would Stewart—or anyone—want to buy another bottled water company?

Back at the house, Stewart organized a blind tasting of about twenty bottles of water, including the top sellers. I performed my tasting trick—as he knew I would. "This one tastes better than the others," I said. A look of smug satisfaction crept over Stewart's face—a ridiculous, immature, and utterly annoying look known by every woman whose husband has just proved her wrong. He announced that the water I had singled out was FIJI brand. And he wanted to buy it.

This was all new to me. Up to that point, I had barely registered the existence of FIJI Water or even the island paradise that produces it. I never drank enough water. When I did, I usually spiked it with POM or something else to make it less boring. FIJI was different. I liked the taste, and I could drink it all day without doctoring it.

The brand had been around for only eight years. Still, it had made considerable progress in a very crowded field, especially in "on premise" work, meaning restaurants and hotels. "On premise" is a critical arena for beverages; it's where many consumers are first introduced to your brand

and where they develop associations between your brand and the experience (hopefully a superlative one) of fine dining or elegant leisure that a good restaurant, hotel, or spa induces. However, volume sales of water are built through grocery stores and mass retailers, not on premise. At the high end of the market, where it competed, FIJI was getting clobbered by Evian, the premium retail giant.

In spite of my misgivings, I knew Stewart's genius in spotting businesses with huge potential. To give you an idea of how good he is with numbers, he can actually help our granddaughter Scarlett do her fourth-grade math homework—and he has the patience to explain it well enough that she can do it herself the next time. Stewart also understands value—and he was certain FIJI had it.

We negotiated with FIJI founder David Gilmour, a wonderful character who combined the finesse of Fred Astaire with the grit of Gary Cooper. After making a fortune in land, gold mines, and who knows what, David bought his own island in Fiji. There, he fell in love with the precious water from an underground aquifer on a neighboring island. It wasn't long before I was packing a bathing suit and floppy hats.

To get the lay of the land, I took what was purported to be a forty-five-minute helicopter tour of the islands. Weather comes up rather unexpectedly in that part of the tropics, and our little flight extended to three and a half hours while we were stuck in a monsoon. In order to keep the interior of the vintage whirlybird from fogging up, the pilot kept the windows open throughout the storm. I got a firsthand look at Fiji's 322 islands, including stunning waterfalls and foliage. I emerged from the helicopter looking like a hysterical middle-aged contestant in a wet T-shirt contest, not the best way to make a great impression on the plant employees who were on hand to get a first look at me.

After months of negotiating—something for which Stewart has the stomach but I don't—we finally bought the company. My mission was to increase sales in every channel. The first step, as always, was to think inside the box—to look within the brand itself for creative solutions to marketing challenges. I don't believe in makeovers for the sake of makeovers, nor do I feel compelled to put my personal stamp on every element of every brand. My staff and I have enough to do already without creating busy work. Before we made any moves with our new liquid asset, there was research to be done; we would need to learn everything there was to know about water.

We assembled a great team of marketing and sales professionals, and together we dipped into the well of information on the various sources of water and the ways in which companies treated, packaged, and delivered it to consumers. We wanted to understand the products and the market, which provides America with more than eight billion gallons a year.

Part of this rigor has to do with logistics. Unfortunately, much of it has to do with health as well, because you can no longer trust public or private water supplies. One of the many downsides of a compromised ecosystem is that microbes, pesticides, and other contaminants have leached into our groundwater. At the same time, airborne pollutants have contaminated the water that falls as rain—so water often gets spiked with pollution literally coming and going.

A 1999 test by the Natural Resources Defense Council found that hundreds of samples of bottled water contained bacterial or chemical contaminants, including carcinogens. According to *Reader's Digest*, even water from a well near a hazardous waste site was bottled and sold. As water shortages grow more serious in some parts of the country, local governments are adopting some truly drastic measures. Orange County, California, has built a $481 million plant to process and purify local sewage into drinking water. It doesn't get much scarier than that.

Making matters worse, many regions have aging water pipes leading from reservoirs and aqueducts to homes. Even New York City's tap water, once the pride of the Big Apple, has deteriorated in recent decades due to increased development in the Catskills region of upstate New York, from which the city draws its supply. I can remember the days when I first had enough money to visit New York and stay in style, instead of crashing on a friend's sofa. After taking a taxi from the airport to the Regency, I would rush up to my room, turn on the faucet, and, while standing over the sink, gulp down the delicious, cold, distinctly New York water. Sadly, as the quality of the water steadily declined, I took to drinking bottled water on my visits, forgoing a mouthful of increasingly chlorinated and sickly softened tap water.

In Europe, the infrastructure is even older and municipal water is even more dubious, which is why bottled water was introduced there before it developed a market here. Europeans live on bottled water—except for those who live on bottled wine.

In America, nearly half the bottled water is purified water that originates with municipal water systems. In other words, it's tap water. Aquafina, Dasani, and Smart Water are three of the most common brands. Basically, everything that occurs naturally in water—minerals and the like—is stripped away, and what's left is a kind of lifeless fluid without any discernible qualities. Some companies add back some of what they take out—but in a chemical, not naturally occurring, form. If not properly pH-balanced, it leaches salts, minerals, and bromides from your body, which is why you can actually overdose on it and go into shock. In a tragic case in California, a woman who had competed in a water-drinking contest actually died.

Nearly all the rest of the bottled water on the market is spring water. There was a time when spring water in America was uniformly pure and delicious, but not in this lifetime. Because springs generally lie just beneath the surface, ground pollutants can, and increasingly do, leach into the supply. Which brings us to the Unique Selling Proposition of FIJI Water.

FIJI Water isn't just a brand name; the water actually comes from a remote island in Fiji, thousands of miles from the nearest industrialized society. However, early research suggested that nobody believed it. We tried to have a little fun and educate consumers at the same time with a simple slogan: "The label says Fiji because it's not bottled in Cleveland." We should have known that the city of Cleveland would not find this humorous. We ruffled a few feathers and suffered a short boycott by the local newspapers for making fun of their fair city.

Our water is a renewable resource, supplied by the monsoon rains. It actually comes from an artesian aquifer on the edge of a Fijian rain forest, deep beneath the earth's surface. As the Environmental Protection Agency and others have pointed out, water from artesian aquifers is protected from contamination by confining layers of rock. Rainwater seeps through the rock over hundreds of years, but the rock acts as a barrier to pollutants. Consequently, water from artesian aquifers is purer than spring water. On this Fijian island, water from the aquifer is a whole different level of pure.

FIJI Water actually fell as rain hundreds of years ago, before the Industrial Revolution. The water filtered through the volcanic rock for two hundred years or so before settling into its ancient aquifer deep within the earth. This natural filtration system does more than protect FIJI Water from the evils of contamination; it adds tremendous benefits. As the water filters through the rock, it acquires mineral silica, which helps build strong bones, hair, skin, and connective tissue and gives FIJI Water its distinctive soft feel in the mouth. FIJI also has more naturally occurring fluoride than any other bottled water.

The aquifer is active—a moving liquid repository. We tap into it by boring deep inside the volcanic rock. The wa-

The source of FIJI's artesian water.

ter is siphoned through hermetically sealed pipes, which channel it directly into the bottle in a totally protected environment. There are no people present. This water comes from deep underground and is utterly untouched by man until you unscrew the cap.

Remember the old Stewart Resnick mantra? "The management is good. I'll let them run the business and it won't take any time from me at all." Right!

FIJI founder David Gilmour stayed on after the sale, as did the company president, but within a few months the old regime was gone. We moved the offices from lovely but inconvenient Aspen to Los Angeles, where we could take advantage of the various benefits of cohabitation with our other companies. Then, based on our new understanding of FIJI Water's Unique Selling Proposition, I set out to change the identity of the brand—while those who had created the original identity cringed.

I try not to be insensitive, but when you have invested $150 million in a company with the intent of taking it to the next level, a little insensitivity is sometimes hard to avoid. Seemingly unaware of FIJI Water's unique aquifer, the existing label on the bottle was a cartoon illustration of a waterfall. Yes, it was a picture of fresh, pristine water rushing over a dramatic cliff in the tropics. Yes, it evoked a sense of unspoiled nature and primitive beauty. Yes, it had a certain allure. But surface water? *Surface* water! Why would you want to suggest that FIJI came from surface water? The waterfall absolutely had to go.

In addition to the waterfall on the front of the label, the existing bottle had a back label that attempted to show where the islands of Fiji are located. The graphics were so weak that it was hard to understand what exactly was being communicated. In addition to these particular issues, there was a more general problem; the bottle was so discreet, so subtle, and so pale it just about disappeared on the supermarket shelf—it was indistinguishable from the background. In some refrigerated cases, which put a frost on the bottle, you couldn't find it with a magnifying glass and a bloodhound. It seemed we had just bought the *Where's Waldo?* of the packaging world.

One great lesson I've learned in retail is to take a mock-up of your product to the point of sale and look at it in its natural habitat—the jungle of competition. We photograph the tableau, take it back to the office, and study what the picture says. Your package at the point of sale is a minibillboard for your brand. You must use that space effectively to communicate your product's virtues, outshine your competitors, and reassure consumers that they are making the right choice when they select your product. I can't tell you how many times I have been surprised by those in situ photographs. Often, the package I loved at close range in the office wasn't the design that worked best on the shelf.

> Your package at the point of sale is a minibillboard
> for your brand.

We revised the front label of the FIJI bottle to make it clear that the water actually comes from Fiji. We used a photo of a lovely hibiscus, just like those that grow around our bottling plant, retaining the charming 3-D effect of the original bottle but replacing the waterfall with palm fronds.

The back labels became central to the marketing plan. There are now six different back labels, each supporting a different element of our Unique Selling Proposition, hopefully with a bit of charm. The first depicts and explains our artesian aquifer. The second places the Fiji islands in context—miles away from the nearest industrialized society. The third tells the story of our slogan: "Untouched by Man." The fourth explains how FIJI's unique mineral profile makes it the best-tasting water. The fifth and sixth labels explain our "green water" approach to sustainability.

As we had done with POM, we made FIJI available at happening parties, health events (like Race for the Cure), and corporate symposia while seeking a close association with movie stars, fashion models, political leaders, and the intelligentsia. But we never use a paid celebrity promoter or spokesperson. I'm thrilled to see a photograph of Nicole Kidman holding a bottle of FIJI or a *Los Angeles Times* photo of Oscar winners Tilda Swinton and Joel Coen clutching their FIJI bottles in one hand and their statues in the other—we all love glamorous movie stars. But we're not in the movie business. Our product is water—and we want the focus on our product.

There is an enormous difference between a product that celebrities love and a product that they are paid to *pretend* they love. Any marketer who thinks consumers are too dumb to notice that gap—and understand what it means—is fooling himself. (Yes, I'm talking to you, Domino's Pizza, but you've got plenty of company.) So why does Nike pay LeBron James a fortune to promote sneakers? Because LeBron James doesn't just get his picture taken with a pair of high-tops; he wears Nike sneakers to work each day—and he works in front of millions of people. Why did Smart Water pay Jennifer Aniston $10 million to hold a bottle of its water? I suspect the decision was made after a close examination of the intrinsic value of fortified tap water. Someone probably concluded it wasn't a very compelling proposition on its own.

After buying FIJI, we advertised on select billboards

and in vertical-interest (single subject) magazines, but a lot of our success was due to the events in which we participated—more than 1,500 a year—and we continue to do them. We are more focused on guerrilla and viral tactics than on advertising. It's hard to find an event where our target market is present and FIJI isn't. Just as important, our team works hard to make sure our brand appears in the kind of environments where we belong. We've benefited from a fair amount of product placement in movies, on television, and in magazines.

All of this has paid off. Since we purchased the company in November 2004, the sales of FIJI Water have increased by more than 300 percent, while the industry has grown by about 30 percent in the same period. In 2008, we surpassed Evian to become the leading premium bottled water in the United States. That wouldn't have been possible without a superior product, but it also wouldn't have been possible without smart marketing and sales.

For all its success, however, FIJI Water also illustrates a difficult communications challenge that is unique to this era. It's a challenge with broad implications, which I'll discuss later, but a number of issues are especially relevant to FIJI.

As I mentioned earlier, the market for bottled water owes much of its growth to environmental degradation. It seems to me that the bottled water industry has an even greater responsibility than others to be sensitive to the environment. As custodians of a little sliver of Fijian paradise, we strongly feel that responsibility. We've gone to considerable lengths to make sure we're fulfilling our obligations.

Fiji's reputation as an island paradise is well earned, and not just because the national food is ice cream. When you approach the atoll by air, you see hundreds of islands and the shallow reefs that surround them. The reefs are veritable forests of coral, in both soft and hard formations. Some formations resemble huge Frankenstein brains while others look like elegant Japanese fans dotted with tiny, brightly colored creatures. The tropical colors are magnificent, ranging from orange to green and deep violet.

These spectacular reefs are home to scorpion fish, ghost pipefish, blue-ribbon eels, mantas, hammerheads, and barracudas (not as stylish as the ones back home in L.A. but less hazardous to your health). If ever a quiet little corner of the earth cried out for preservation, Fiji is it.

FIJI Water has brought good jobs and an expanded tax base to the nation. However, given the fragile ecosystem there and the state of the globe in general, we felt we also needed to have a comprehensive environmental policy for our business.

The result is "FIJI Green," a multifaceted sustainability program with the goal of reducing our environmental impact, as well as the amount of carbon we produce. The program is based on ambitious goals and hard commitments to reach them. In 2008, FIJI Water became the first carbon-*negative* beverage on the market.

In addition, we will cut carbon emissions by 25 percent across our product life cycle by 2010. Working with our partner Conservation International, we will continue to invest in reforestation and other carbon reduction projects. These reductions will equal *at least* 120 percent of our carbon production each year. By 2010, 50 percent of our energy needs in Fiji will be derived from renewable sources such as wind and solar.

We are also working with the people of Fiji and Conservation International to protect and preserve the Sovi Basin, the largest lowland rain forest in Fiji. This effort alone will keep ten million tons of carbon out of the atmosphere in perpetuity. That's the equivalent of removing two million passenger cars from the roads for an entire year or planting 500,000 trees. We also contribute to more than one hundred water access projects in Fiji, ensuring that Fijians have access to their own clean water, especially in local schools.

Consumers rightly expect us to be not only environmentally conscious but environmentally *responsive*. The time for good intentions has passed. It's now time for *action*. As environmental issues grow more prominent—and the consequences of pollution more dire—this will become a larger priority for consumers worldwide. Right now, there is a small band of environmentalists in a sea of consumers. It won't be long, however, before the majority of consumers are environmentalists—and the majority of good companies, too.

CHAPTER 7

Eyeballs Ain't Enough

I n recent years, people who buy media have been obsessed with "eyeballs." How many eyeballs does that sitcom deliver? Whose Web site has the most desirable eyeballs? I'm fond of eyeballs myself. I use them regularly. But when I buy media to promote one of our brands, I'm not focused on eyeballs—that's a part of the anatomy that's easily distracted and often glazed over with consumer apathy. I want *hearts and minds.* So I need a message—and ways of using media—that can help us win them.

As it happens, I truly love media of all kinds, but that doesn't mean I like media indiscriminately, and it certainly doesn't mean I want to throw a lot of money at advertising and promotion in the vague hope that something sticks. I don't like media *that* much.

In POM's first four years, we spent a grand total of $14 million on marketing. That includes advertising, promotion, public relations—the works. I can't give you an exact figure detailing how much real communications value we purchased for that relatively small sum, but a conservative estimate is in the hundreds of millions. Every dollar we've invested in researching and understanding our brand has yielded many additional dollars' worth of media attention. I have several binders, all inches thick, filled with newspaper and magazine articles about Wonderful pomegranates and POM. They're the kind of credible, third-party endorsements that money can't buy. All of that priceless, positive buzz helped increase revenue and significantly enhanced our brand equity.

> I'm not focused on eyeballs—that's a part
> of the anatomy that's easily distracted and often
> glazed over with consumer apathy.

We follow the same approach with FIJI Water. If you asked me what the advertising-to-sales ratio is at FIJI Water, I wouldn't be able to tell you. We don't think in terms of set formulas, we instead think in terms of maximizing every investment dollar, doing the most with the least, and staying agile. At all of our companies, we maintain an entrepreneurial culture that enables us to move quickly to seize opportunities. We don't get locked into rigid routines or, worse, narrow mind-sets that limit creativity.

You rarely hear about Marshall McLuhan these days, but he was a brilliant and provocative thinker at least a couple decades ahead of his time. I grew up believing his famous aphorism—"The medium is the message"—only to discover through trial and error that the truth is a bit more complicated. The medium *shapes* the message, the medium *qualifies* the message, it can even *alter* the message—but the medium itself is not the message.

Messages are important, and, like most important things, it takes time to do them right. When I sit down with my team, our goal is to devise a message that is concise, direct, and immediately accessible. That doesn't mean I'm looking for a blunt instrument—more like a surgeon's scalpel. Above all, we're looking for a message that delivers on two distinct levels: we want it to be authentic, and we want it to register on the brain. The message has to be memorable.

Our POM campaign provides a number of excellent examples. We don't focus on extraneous plot lines or attributes. We treat our POM bottle as the hero of every ad. The iconic bottle is probably what catches your eye and draws you to the product in the first place; its organic form is an invitation to drop it into your shopping cart. In fact, the bottle has so much personality that we actually put a superhero cape on it and called it the "Antioxidant Superhero." Another POM example, perhaps our best known, likewise consisted of just two words: "Cheat Death." When you see that brave little bottle with a noose around its neck—a noose broken by the antioxidant power of POM—you identify with it just as you identify with a hero's triumph or last-minute escape from danger on the movie screen.

Empathy is a powerful social adhesive, so we try to elicit that natural feeling for our product/hero. When talking to our young female audience, we show the POM bottle under a hair dryer with the headline "Extreme Makeover." The audience understands that POM antioxidants make you over from the inside out. If we can make you chuckle, we have an opportunity to connect with a more serious message grounded in our brand's identity and intrinsic value. We can also go too far. When we used an image of a POM bottle in a bridal veil with the message "Outlive your spouse," it took only a few complaints posted on our message board for me to pull the campaign. I realized that for some people, it could never be funny.

Brevity is an essential principle of message creation. Remember Tom Peters's slogan from the late 1980s? "Keep it simple, stupid." Consumers didn't have the patience for a harangue then, and they have even less tolerance for one today. If your message is a paragraph long, you need to go back to the drawing board because you don't have a message—you have a paragraph. A concise, potent message travels well. You can publish it in a magazine and mount it on a billboard. You can put it on a Web site or embroider it on a baseball cap. The shorter the message, the more easily it adapts to different circumstances—and the more readily it travels between different media.

> If your message is a paragraph long, you don't have a message—you have a paragraph.

At best, most advertising skims the surface of our consciousness before we move right past it. That's hardly surprising. Estimates of the number of messages the average consumer confronts vary from about 250 to 5,000 a day. The low range is overwhelming; the high range is downright abusive. A recent report by the market research firm Yankelovich put a hard number on a common assumption: it found that 69 percent of Americans expressed interest "in ways to block, skip or opt out of being exposed to advertising."

Successful advertising makes us register the moment and take notice. If you can generate a reaction in consumers, you've already achieved a major goal; you've become a part of their life in that small but very critical moment. If you use that moment to land a solid message somewhere on the brain—a message grounded in your brand identity and value—then you've truly achieved a great deal.

Whatever you say in your ad and however you deliver the message, it had better be true. Don't put yourself—or your product—in the position of selling old-fashioned lemonade with no lemons in it.

If you're Ford or Procter & Gamble, I guess you see the benefit of spending tens of millions of dollars on thirty-second television spots, but the value of that approach has never been so obvious to me. According to Jeffrey Cole at the USC Annenberg School Center for the Digital Future, television viewers actually watch only between 5 and 10 percent of the commercials on TV. It's astounding but true.

More people than ever are watching TV; they just aren't watching commercials. I don't want to spend exorbitant sums to reach a television audience that has recorded a show on TiVo and is merrily skipping all the spots. It's pointless to shout at a consumer who just got up from the sofa to get a beer from the fridge or to put her child to bed. I don't want to try to interrupt a consumer who is talking to his spouse about paying the mortgage, and I'm not at all interested in reaching a video zombie who has been channel surfing for hours on end, zipping by dozens of commercials, all of which have begun to run together in the creature's increasingly mushy mind. We haven't given up on television altogether. We are running some outlandish thirty-second spots on late-night shows with some positive results.

The one place where television spots resonate sometimes even more than the content is on the Super Bowl. And at three million dollars for a thirty-second spot the creative better be outstanding and memorable. If consumers respond to your message these commercials can have a second life in traditional media where they become news and are shown over and over again on TV and the Internet. Three million dollars. At that price, it had better be a good one.

Billboards

Billboards may not be glamorous, but you can't TiVo your way through a billboard. In fact, the only way to miss a well-placed billboard is to drive with your eyes closed (much like the passengers in the backseat of my car). Of course, coming up with a memorable billboard ad isn't easy, but this isn't about easy—it's about effective.

The only way to miss a well-placed billboard is to drive with your eyes closed.

Outdoor advertising is relatively cheap, although some locations are cheap for good reason. When you buy, keep in mind the old Reagan policy of "trust, but verify"—then throw out the "trust" part. We never buy sight unseen. Instead, we travel the city (*every* city) analyzing the best locations and making sure we're not buying a location with an obstructed view or some other undesirable attribute. We buy only premium locations, including cityscapes and wallscapes. We buy bulletins—large, illuminated, glowing boards that charge a big premium—whenever possible; they're the gold standard of outdoor advertising and are worth it. If we can get an extension on top so the image of our bottle literally rises above the city, we take it.

We keep our headlines simple and short—five words or less. One can absorb only a short burst of language at thirty-five miles per hour. We pay close attention to lighting. When we were introducing POM, I naively bought ad space in a bunch of telephone kiosks in Manhattan. Later, on a trip to the city, I kept looking for our ads but couldn't find them. Why? I hadn't bought illuminated kiosks, and by 4:00 p.m. on a winter day, they had disappeared into the darkness. It was a dumb mistake I never made again. Telephone kiosks are a great buy but only if you buy the Rolls-Royce of the line, the illuminated ones that glow through traffic 24/7.

There are some wild things you can do with outdoor advertising to cover a city for very little money. In introducing POM Coffee to Los Angeles and New York City, we wanted blanket coverage with a zany spirit reflective of the new brand. While transit postings and subway lines are a staple of ours, this time we experimented with mobile billboards, bus wraps, wild postings (numerous posters on deserted buildings, construction fences, etc.), taxi tops, sandwich boards, college kiosks and newspapers, bar coasters, and even posters placed on the wall above the toilets in select bars (talk about the concentration of your audience). The success of a launch in a big city can replicate itself as you roll out across the country, giving you a retail story to tell in each successive market.

There's nothing random about the way we buy. We want visibility in areas with high commuter density and in neighborhoods with a concentration of our target audience. Commuter rails and subway cars are a great way to get exposure in cities with large commuter populations. We may appear in only a few locations, but our target consumers see us everywhere: on their way to work, in the neighborhoods, where they live, where they shop, where they go out to dinner, where they meet their friends, creating different points of contact throughout the day. Despite limited resources and select locations, we still manage to achieve an effect of ubiquity. "I see your billboards everywhere," people tell me.

One of the many benefits of doing all our work inhouse is that we're able to build the kind of relationships with vendors that are usually the exclusive province of ad agencies. And once in a while, we call in a favor. When Teleflora participated in a big campaign in which we donated 20 percent of sales on select bouquets to the fight against breast cancer, our key outdoor vendor helped us out with $500,000 worth of free billboards to support the campaign. Because our staff cares deeply about our mission—and about the charities we support—they take the time to convince others to care as well.

Newspapers

Print's heyday may have been the nineteenth and twentieth centuries, when newspapers and magazines proliferated, but I still adore the feel of the *New York Times* in my hands on a twenty-first century Sunday morning. No other medium is as tactile, portable, and immediate (and messy), allowing readers to linger over an article—or an ad—at their leisure, tear it out, and put it in their pocket for future reference.

When we owned the Franklin Mint, we had one of the largest magazine budgets in the advertising business, in excess of $300 million a year. We learned to negotiate directly with publications. Agencies, which get a commission on the total buy, have no incentive to negotiate lower rates, but we insist on getting value for our money—and vendors know we're willing to walk away if we don't get a fair price. When you add up what we save by avoiding agency fees and negotiating directly with vendors, it's a lot of money.

In the late 1980s and early '90s, the Franklin Mint was

the biggest advertiser in *Parade* magazine, the weekly delivered in Sunday newspapers. Because the Mint thrived on direct response, we needed a heavy and regular advertising presence. At the time, *Parade* had upward of 45 million readers and a weekly delivery schedule as sure as clockwork, making it an ideal vehicle for us. Learning the business through direct response was like running a research firm dedicated to measuring the effectiveness of print advertising. With direct response, you *know* if the publication is pulling in readers—you can count the coupons that accompany the checks. Alas, today *Parade* has a fraction of the pages it once had, and it no longer delivers the same response.

Today, the average reader of a big-city newspaper is sixty years old. When older readers die, they aren't being replaced. People simply get their news from too many other sources, including the Internet and TV. The average young consumer today doesn't have a relationship with a newspaper and doesn't seem to have the time or interest to develop one.

Nevertheless, in large metro Sunday papers, free-standing inserts (the coupons touting savings on everything from food to cleaning products and collector coins) are still a great deal. They aren't exactly sexy and they don't do much for your brand image, but they can entice consumers to give your brand a try. Without a trial, you don't get the second purchase that means so much. We use free-standing inserts for Teleflora holiday bouquets, with a discount coupon consumers can redeem online or at their local flower shop. POM, FIJI Water, and our Everybody's Nuts brand of pistachios are also frequent advertisers.

Despite their decline, I think that newspapers in small cities are still a viable medium. Millions of people rely on their local paper for everything from high school sports news to supermarket sales notices. There is a community spirit evident in a good local newspaper that can't be imitated by national media. Local news is always important news. I always read the local *Aspen Times* when I'm vacationing at our family home there. I like the sense of community it embodies, and I'm eager to know what's going on around town: movies, gossip, sales, and new restaurant openings. Local papers offer not only good value but real eyeballs that want to see what's being offered.

Magazines

Vertical-interest magazines remain an extremely valuable part of the media mix. Like newspapers, they're tactile, but they're also glossy and colorful, immersed in celebrity and pop culture. Women's magazines, health magazines, celebrity magazines such as *Shape, People, Us Weekly, OK,* and *In Touch* are all on our list. Sure, they've been running the same stories—"10 Minutes to Flatter Abs" and "Starlet Dates Bad Boy"—since the Neanderthals were a hot gossip item, but, hey, it seems to work. Also, when we see glossy photos of celebs holding FIJI Water, we know that's an environment in which we want to advertise.

Here again, our in-house operations give us an advantage. When we hear about a great remnant—which, like a carpet remnant, is always had at a discount—we move on it immediately without relying on the cumbersome machinery of an ad agency. Who knows if an agency would even bother to tell us about it?

Agencies are not conducive to speed. Is the account executive at the agency out to lunch? Making a pitch to a client? Who knows? Has the client's magazine budget already been spent? If it has, is the account exec going to pry new funds from the client to buy an unplanned ad at a discount? Not without a conference call and multiple deliberations. By the time a decision comes down, the ad space is long gone. I know, because I probably bought it.

When we are offered a quality magazine placement at a great rate, we take it. If a new expense is not in the budget, we change the budget to accommodate it.

We have a number of parameters that guide our magazine and ad buys:

1. We want the right-hand page, forward in the book.
2. No full-page ad opposite our ad.
3. No coupon on the back side of our ad.

For the right price, we'll give up all of those demands—except one. Our ad must appear on the right-hand page; that's the page that draws the eye even as the hand turns the page. No right hand, no business.

Radio

Radio is fundamentally a promotional medium. We don't advertise on radio, but we do promote there. I believe only in local radio—and only when we can work out a promotional campaign that's integrated into a show's content. We want listeners to hear about our product from the deejay they specifically tune in to hear. And we want to be included in the show's format—not outside it in the form of a "commercial break." We've had success working with top deejays, such as some of the Spanish-language radio stars in Miami, who have devoted followings and can introduce a brand with credibility and verve, generating excitement with contests and prizes. Today, it is all about content—and you want to be a part of it, not an add-on.

> **Radio is fundamentally a promotional medium.**

That's one of the reasons we love National Public Radio. NPR's *Morning Edition*, for instance, delivers an audience of 12.7 million people every day. These are civic-minded, influential citizens who vote, recycle, and care deeply about the planet, all qualities reflected in our brands. Now, you can't run a thirty- or sixty-second spot with a jingle, but I love to sponsor a segment because you become integrated with the content of the show. Your brand is gilded by association.

Product Placement

Similarly, we like to see our products in hit television shows and films. When someone on Wisteria Lane opens a refrigerator, you might see a bottle of POM or FIJI Water cooling on the shelf. Our products appear on *House, Heroes, Boston Legal, Scrubs, Friends with Money, CSI: Miami, Nip/Tuck,* and *Grey's Anatomy,* to name a few. This is hardly a new tactic. Back in the fifties, the Nelson family drank milk by the gallon on *The Adventures of Ozzie and Harriet,* which was sponsored by the American Dairy Association. We use product placement in part because it tips off our consumers—and target market—that they're "in the know." Getting great exposure for the cost of the product and a modest retainer paid to our product placement firm warms my heart and heats up the bottom line.

To make our mark at the cineplex, we worked our way into *Traveling,* a Jennifer Aniston film in which she plays a florist. We designed the bouquet her character arranges and then made it possible for our Teleflora florists to design and deliver the same bouquet. As the film business struggles and television viewership continues to fracture, producers realize that product placement is a viable revenue source and marketers like us still appreciate the rich combination of celebrity and seemingly organic environments. Most Sony films today include Sony electronics—stereos, televisions, computers—meticulously placed in select scenes. Characters may even pass ads for Sony products when they walk down the street. If the placement is handled poorly, it can look like a clumsy attempt at subliminal advertising, but when it is organic to context and setting, it works.

We've also been experimenting with running viral videos in art-house theaters. The spots have to be uniquely compelling—either charming or hysterically funny—for this gambit to succeed, but it's well worth a try.

Event Marketing and Promotion

Most of our marketing energy is focused not on advertising but on a wide range of viral activity. One of the most important lessons I've learned over the years is also one of the most counterintuitive: if you want to make money on a product, you have to learn how to give it away. FIJI Water is waiting at the finish line for the parched runner who has just completed a marathon. POM is in the gift bag at a high-profile celebrity event. We give thousands of Teleflora coupons away during the year.

Why give it away? You can't get a consumer to try your product twice if she hasn't had it once. We're all creatures of habit; some of us need a little extra incentive to try something new. Giving away your product shows you have confidence in it. It means you're convinced that if consumers try it once for free, they'll be willing to pay for it next time. That doesn't mean you give it away randomly. You need to choose the right events with the right consumers and the right atmosphere.

> If you want to make money on a product, you have to learn how to give it away.

We hired Dale DeGroff, the King of Cocktails, to develop a signature drink for the Academy Awards, Golden Globes, and Emmys, and the POMtini cocktail was born. It was such a hit that the Motion Picture Academy made it the official cocktail of the Oscars in 2003, 2004, and 2005. (In 2006, Coca-Cola, the 1,500-pound gorilla of the beverage industry, muscled into the show and everyone else was kicked out.)

We sent a team across the country to teach bartenders at top restaurants and bars how to make the POMtini. Great restaurants from coast to coast now feature pomegranate drinks on their bar menus. Consumers can find recipes for more than fifty drinks (with and sans alcohol) on our Web site.

Our efforts extend far beyond Hollywood. Each year, we send a gorgeous, hardbound coffee-table book on POM to editors and producers. The book, filled with history, recipes, and lush photography, is so expensive to produce it makes me shudder, but I also know that it conveys just how serious we are about our product. Last year, in an effort to advance our green initiative, we made a major push on the digital version of our press kit. (Look for the old press kits on eBay—they are true keepsakes.)

We make a point of sending POM to a long list of influential people, including doctors, celebrities, politicians, and media industry leaders. Years ago, I met Martha Stewart at a prostate cancer event. There was a workshop that day for the golf widows, who were kept busy making glass coasters. Martha taught us how. She was kind enough not to mention how disgraceful my handiwork was, but she did mention to me that she loved pomegranates. I paid attention. And each year at the beginning of our harvest, I send her a case of our Wonderful pomegranates with my compliments. I never expected anything to come of it, but was happy to nurture and encourage her enthusiasm for my favorite fruit. After all, she is Queen of Homemaking.

Some years later, Martha did a beautiful twelve-page spread on pomegranates in *Martha Stewart Living*. The following year, her television show filmed a segment featuring yours truly touring the orchards. In subsequent years, she has featured pomegranates when the season begins. Did my annual gift have anything to do with it? Probably not. By her own admission, Martha is crazy for pomegranates. But I know that at least once a year she is reminded of how much she likes them.

Of course, not everyone has the chance to meet Martha Stewart, but anyone can send a product to someone who is influential—whether it's the editor of a local newspaper or the head of the chamber of commerce. It probably won't result in an avalanche of sales, but you never know.

Having your product adopted by an influential person has its own rewards. After all, leaders have followers. In every city, there are charity events where you can have a coupon for your service or a sample of your product included in the goody bag that guests take home. I first discovered the mineral foundation makeup to which I have been faithful for five years now in a gift bag. So don't be stingy. Sharing your product shows confidence—and builds it, too.

Public Relations

Old media, new media—who cares? Just get mentioned in the media—that's what counts. Public relations is the unsung hero of marketing. There is nothing as effective in the entire world as getting someone else to say something good about your product or service—what we call "third-party endorsement." Of course, POM is newsworthy. First, the press loved us because the fruit was so new yet so old, and the health story was a revelation. As time went on, we became the darling of food editors when our fresh season started. We have new medical breakthroughs on a regular basis, so there is always something new and exciting to learn about POM.

Everything we've achieved has been done in-house, starting with one great public relations veteran. That was about five years ago. Today, we have public relations executives in each business dedicated to building our brands on TV and radio and in print. We have garnered hundreds of millions of dollars' worth of publicity through these efforts.

> Public relations is the unsung hero of marketing.

In addition to being featured on all the great cooking shows, we have become a staple on the morning news, with pomegranate recipes and decorating tips, but above all with medical breakthroughs from POM Wonderful. You can't beat that kind of exposure for brand building, with credible, third-party endorsements—no matter how much money you spend.

I'm going to discuss the WWW (that's either the World Wide Web or the Wild, Wild West) in the next chapter. I think the mysteries and minefields of the Internet merit a separate discussion all their own, but first, I want to briefly describe a kind of marketing test case, a campaign that integrated many of the strategies and tactics that I've just described in pursuit not of random eyeballs but of genuine hearts and minds.

TELEFLORA'S CONTEST TO CROWN America's Favorite Mom took more than a year of planning, multiple rounds of painstaking negotiation, seemingly endless hours of work, and millions of dollars of investment. But it was worth it.

"America's Favorite Mom" integrated television, Internet, print, and on-premises promotion in 21,000 florist shops to produce a marketing phenomenon tied to the hundredth anniversary of Mother's Day on May 11, 2008. The full name of the show was "Teleflora Presents America's Favorite Mom." Now, *that* is product placement—or, as I call it, Product Programming Integration.

Growing up in Hollywood as the daughter of a film producer, I was fully aware of the disappointment club that we call "the Industry." I never did want to be part of that ego-destroying affair. The reason I created "America's Favorite Mom" wasn't to become a TV executive, it was to make the Teleflora brand stronger with our target market and to sell beautifully arranged flowers in our keepsake container for the holiday. Most important, we wanted to communicate that Teleflora is the first name in flowers. To that end, we wanted to own the most important holiday in the floral industry: Mother's Day.

We started in April 2007, more than a year before the centenary, by traveling to a small West Virginia church. That's where Anna Jarvis first gave out flowers to the moms in the congregation in honor of her mother's memory. It was the nation's first celebration of Mother's Day.

We purchased the rights to tell the story of the founding and, for goodwill, helped out with a new organ for the church, because we wanted to include the church and its people in our celebration. But we also wanted the rights for another reason: because whether the subject is pomegranates, pearls, or Mother's Day, authenticity matters.

Having been around Hollywood so long, I knew that

striking the right television deal would require a lot of patience and persistence. Who was I kidding? I didn't know the half of it. After bringing in a first-rate producing partner, Reveille Productions, which is responsible for hits such as *The Office, Ugly Betty,* and *The Biggest Loser,* we proceeded to negotiate with NBC. Ben Silverman, the network's head of programming, immediately understood our vision for the special, but it took six long months to get the deal done through the network's legal department. It was excruciating at times, but we kept faith with our vision and eventually we had the makings of great television.

> Whether the subject is pomegranates, pearls, or Mother's Day, authenticity matters.

The premise of Teleflora's program was easily grasped: a celebration of American moms, all 82 million of us. But the number of moving parts was daunting. The campaign included: (1) our own dedicated and separate Web site (something the network rarely agrees to) for user-generated nominations for the title of America's Favorite Mom; (2) a five-day salute on NBC's top-rated *Today* show, with each of the five segments celebrating a different type of mom, such as single mom, working mom, or military mom (since *Today* is part of the network's news division and our special was entertainment, it required those two departments to work together); and (3) an hour-long, prime-time grand finale special on Mother's Day 2008, hosted by Donny and Marie Osmond, on which America's Favorite Mom was selected. (The eventual winner, Patty Patton-Bader, received $250,000, a new kitchen from GE, a family vacation in the Caribbean, flowers for a year from Teleflora, and a solid gold America's Favorite Mom pendant rimmed with brilliant diamonds.)

We developed a beautiful spring bouquet in a lustrous pink keepsake vase. The special bouquet was decorated with a lovely golden heart-shaped pendant attached, similar to the one America's Favorite Mom received. That way, everyone in America could purchase the bouquet and tell their mom that, in their eyes, she was their favorite.

We bought additional print advertising, created an outdoor ad campaign, did radio in select markets and made a huge PR push to be sure the maximum number of people knew about "America's Favorite Mom" and wanted to be a part of it.

On the Web, MySpace, which supports more than ninety million unique visits daily, was our social networking partner. Our site enabled video nominations of moms to be uploaded, viewed, and shared, along with testimonials and all manner of mom discussion. A special page was dedicated to essays on moms. We developed our own videos and seeded them on YouTube. Two of these videos—"Mom Simulator" and "Rock for Mom"—made it (organically) to YouTube's home page, the holy grail of viral media.

Most important, our 21,000 Teleflora member florists

were integral to the whole operation. In addition to selling the bouquets for the hundredth anniversary, they promoted the contest in their shops with special merchandising and an "America's Favorite Mom" marketing kit that we distributed. The florists themselves competed to produce the most eye-catching displays, with a winner in each state receiving about $1,000 in merchandise and a chance to enter a sweepstakes to win a new delivery van. Our florists processed "mominations" and delivered special "America's Favorite Mom" bouquets all across the country.

"America's Favorite Mom" was an enormously powerful marketing campaign, yet it cost us less than the price of an average television advertising buy. In fact, for what we spent on "America's Favorite Mom," we could not possibly have bought a TV advertising campaign that would have delivered real impact. Instead, we got a nationwide phenomenon that incorporated a full week of national network television, encompassing forty-five minutes of content on the top-rated morning show; a terrific interactive presence on the Web sites of MySpace, Teleflora, and "America's Favorite Mom" (the "America's Favorite Mom" Web site alone received 800,000 visits); promotional support from *Redbook,* one of America's most popular women's magazines; and a bricks-and-mortar promotion at 21,000 florist shops throughout the United States. It was integrated from top to bottom, and that doesn't even count all the press and public relations value generated as a result of this confluence of forces. What's more, we ran the whole operation with a small staff out of our offices in Los Angeles.

"Teleflora Presents America's Favorite Mom" was never intended to capture eyeballs. It went right for the heart of the matter. Does the English language contain a word more emotionally resonant than "mom"? Is there any group more deserving of celebration and reward than mothers?

Our moms got attention. Patricia Griffith, one of our Working Mom finalists, was approached by the Food Network about doing a show. Nora Leon, our Adopting Mom winner, saw interest in her work in Haiti increase dramatically. She was even contacted by musician Wyclef Jean about getting involved. Other featured moms attracted interest as well, suggesting that the programming really touched lives.

At every level, the "America's Favorite Mom" campaign met our criteria for marketing. It was grounded in authenticity. It targeted hearts and minds. It used multiple media and multiple platforms to support the campaign. It was a creative breakthrough that originated in-house and was achieved through promotion, PR, and innovative communications—not through expensive, wasteful thirty-second TV spots or generic national radio spots.

The results? We sold a record number of keepsake products. Sales of our "star" bouquet were up 90 percent over the previous year. And we rallied our florist network around a concept that benefited us all, paving the way for tighter collaboration in the future.

Marketers constantly say they are eager to "break through the clutter," to somehow get noticed amid the bombardment of commercial messages that assaults the average American consumer each and every day. But though everyone says they want to break through the clutter, many are afraid to do so; they feel more comfortable doing pretty much the same thing that everyone else is doing. In other words, they'd rather join the clutter than shatter it.

If you really want to break through, you first have to break out of decades of media habits that are no longer relevant. The old ways may still get you lots of eyeballs, but is that really all you want? Success in this environment requires a real connection to hearts and minds. Eyeballs ain't enough.

CHAPTER 8

Web of Wonder
(and Deceit)

1. The Internet is the greatest communications advance since Johannes Gutenberg invented movable type.
2. The Internet is a web of deception, half-truths, bias, spin, and pornography, both metaphoric and actual.

Which statement is true?

It's clear you could summon an army of evidence to support either view. But the two statements aren't mutually exclusive. The Internet *is* the greatest communications advance since the printing press, enabling rapid, inexpensive communication between individuals and groups around the world. It's also full of more lies and phony elixirs than a snake oil salesman's carnival wagon.

I have been working in cyberspace since the late 1990s, when I designed the first Franklin Mint Web site selling collectibles online. A few years later, Teleflora began selling direct to consumers over the Internet. Meanwhile, a subtle transformation had been taking shape all around me. I was unable to define exactly what was going on, but it felt a lot like the sand eroding beneath my feet on Malibu Beach. Everything I had learned about communications and marketing was shifting. The rules were changing, and I didn't have a firm grip on how to apply my knowledge to this new paradigm. Then it hit me. This was the first time since Julius Caesar addressed the people of Rome (slaves and women not included) that society could engage in a genuine two-way dialogue. Citizens were talking back—to government, to corporate America, and to each other, and they were doing it worldwide in real time. As *Time* put it in 2006, when "You" became the magazine's Person of the Year: "It's a chance for people to look at a computer screen and really, genuinely wonder who's out there looking back at them."

We all understand that the Internet is a transformational communications medium. But the old advertising ways, which easily morphed from print to radio to television as each new technology was introduced, have somehow stumbled with the onset of the Internet.

That's in part because it's not just new, it's different from its predecessors; a medium for a new world with new ways that are still being born. Advertisers that try to make the Internet conform to the old paradigms of television or print advertising are often confused and disappointed by the results.

With our brands, we quickly learned we had to adapt our marketing to the medium. As an advertising medium, the Internet is unique. We try to focus on its most compelling assets, which are social and informational.

We begin, not surprisingly, with a Web site. As Alexander King, a now-forgotten writer whom I adored when I was a kid, used to say, "What if the greatest snow skier in the world lived in deepest Africa—no one would ever know." Substitute "product" for "snow skier" and "Internet" for "Africa" and you have the gist of the challenge: How will they find you?

Ever since we first introduced POM, we have put our Web address on every product we sell. Putting your URL on your products is the cheapest and most effective ad spend you can make—because it's free.

Once our consumers locate our Web sites, they are pleasantly surprised by the huge trove of facts about our brands, their history and future, and our point of view on the planet. To give our consumers an easy way of talking back, we offer message boards and blogs that we constantly monitor in order to hear their voices. This enables us to react to issues quickly rather than wait for them to explode in the blogosphere.

One of the greatest time-saving, money-saving, and truth-telling capabilities of the Internet is its ability to generate accurate market research data. In the old days, market research was expensive and time-consuming. We used to conduct focus groups in different parts of the country to gauge reactions to a product. Then we'd follow up with field research by telephone or mail. It cost tens of thousands of dollars and took months to compile into meaningful data. By the time you finally received the executive summary of the survey, the information was often dated.

Now we hire a research firm that specializes in online lists, which are easily tailored to the needs of the moment. For a small fee, usually less than $5,000, the firm provides a list of our target audience of consumers. For example, we can request ready-to-drink coffee consumers to test our POMx Coffee or online floral buyers who fit Teleflora's demographic profile.

The results are ready in just days (not weeks or months) and I find them more reliable than the old research data. The time and money saved are considerable; the mistakes we avoid are priceless. But it's also important to remember that research is simply another information tool to help you make a decision. In the end, you still need to use your own instincts and common sense.

For example, when we were creating our campaign for POMx Coffee, research suggested that the phrase "Healthy Buzz" alienated some consumers, who associated the phrase with the drug culture. I listened. But in the end, I decided that the fact that those two words made people pause and think—even sometimes negatively—was okay. First, making people stop and think is the goal of good advertising. Second, no two words better describe what POMx Coffee delivers. We stuck with the language we knew was true.

We use banner ads around the holidays to promote traffic to our Teleflora site. For our other brands, we occasionally buy banners on sites that have a particular synergy with what we stand for. But we have not rushed headlong onto the Web with advertising dollars. In this, we're not alone. Advertising revenue on the Web is rising steadily. But as I write this, less than 10 percent of U.S. advertising is devoted to the Internet. We're at a crossroads of past and future. At the same time that culture and business are scrambling online, a surprising number of corporate executives still have their secretaries print their e-mails. But there is no question about which platforms the future will bless.

Internet users have gradually come to accept that exposure to ads on their favorite sites is the price to be paid for free content. Given that the amount of content on the Web is constantly approaching infinity, it's not a bad deal. But that doesn't mean they're eager to put up with any advertising that comes their way. Pop-ups, for example, are generally poison—although I suspect they may work better in certain contexts than many people think. Blunt, head-on tactics often do—but you won't find an argument for them in this book.

> Internet users have come to accept that exposure to ads on their favorite sites is the price to be paid for free content.

The department store magnate John Wanamaker's lament is perhaps the most famous axiom in the history of advertising. "Half the money I spend on advertising is wasted," he fretted. "The trouble is, I don't know which half." Wanamaker's complaint lingered for a century, vexing advertisers who could no more track the impact of mass advertising in print or on radio or television than Wanamaker could. Thanks to Google and the precision of search, we finally have an answer. If they click, it works. If they don't, it doesn't. We know which half is working.

Despite the relative precision of search, there will always be a bit of mystery to business. Back at the Franklin Mint, Stewart used to complain about the overhead cost of creating 1,500 new products a year. "You only need to roll out five hundred," he would say. Sure, Mr. Wanamaker, but which five hundred?

Teleflora's flowers-in-a-gift concept used to require a similar element of guesswork. Mall intercept studies are the least reliable research tool and very expensive to field, but in the old days that was all we had to test Teleflora's bouquet ideas. ("Madame, I know you have three shopping bags brimming with stuff and your kid is screaming for attention, but which of these bouquet concepts do you like the most?") Now we use the Internet to help us make decisions. Our in-house design team develops more than a hundred concepts for each holiday. We winnow those ideas down to a more manageable number for online testing, then let our consumers tell us which ones they would be most likely to buy.

Search and They Shall Find

THERE ARE three forms of advertising on the Web that I find the most effective; organic search, paid search, and e-mail blasts. The last is self-explanatory: you build an e-mail list over time and regularly send communications to your customers. This form of advertising has a very low cost per order (CPO) and is extremely effective.

Search, however, can be confusing. To understand it, think back to the way some companies used to approach the Yellow Pages. Before that bulky, printed version of search first appeared, there weren't a lot of companies named AA Towing and Acme Lawn Care. But with the Yellow Pages guiding consumers to the goods and services they were seeking, entrepreneurs realized they might get a leg up if their company name appeared at the top of the alphabetical listings. As a result, names beginning in A or even AAA became popular. Internet search adapts the same kind of logic to a new medium.

Why Do We Care About Search Engine Marketing?

"Most online shoppers use search to research before buying," says a new study by Harris Interactive called "How America Searches." In fact, the study tells us that 88 percent of adult online shoppers conduct some form of online research before making a purchase on the Web. Internet search engines are used by 67 percent of these shoppers.

There are two types of **search engine marketing**. First, there is **search engine optimization (SEO)**, which entails adapting your site to improve your chances of appearing more prominently in the organic results of your consumers' search queries. In other words, when someone searches for "pome-granates" on the Web, we want to be certain that POM is the top site they see as a result.

To do it right may take an armchair Einstein, but once you realize how important SEO is, you'll be motivated to find the right Einstein (you needn't have one in-house; such talents are readily outsourced).

Search engines (Google, Ask.com, etc.) **crawl** your Web site, as often as every hour if you are CNN.com or as infrequently as once a month if you are a small site with little traffic. They download your pages and store them, which is why nothing on the Web ever dies.

There are a number of techniques you can use to exploit search engine technology, including creating **meta-tags,** which is background coding on a site that's invisible to consumers; **changing site content** to be more relevant to key search terms; and securing **links to your site from other relevant source sites,** such as official sites in your field or industry (for instance, if you are a breeder of Cavalier King Charles spaniels, make sure you are listed on the American Kennel Club site).

Search engines **index** by extracting information from your site. **Content,** meaning the words on the page, is key. Images and Flash files are not interpreted as words, so they don't count as much, although you can get more out of them by utilizing alternative text for such elements. **Location of keywords is important, so make sure they appear early in page content. Weight** is the frequency with which words are used—so include important words often enough to improve page relevancy. **Links** register all the links included on the page.

By using an **algorithm,** software logic that can identify

and rate the most relevant Web pages, search engines rank information on their sites and determine what information is going to be first, second, or fifty-fourth on a given response to a search request. Sadly, there is no God—and certainly no fairness—governing this process. It is up to the advertiser to know how it works and how to take advantage of every nuance.

Let's say you go to Google and type in the words "dish towels," as I did recently after I realized the ones in my kitchen looked like they had been used to clean up after a pandemic. The clever sites that had seeded their home pages with dish towel information—information discovered by the search engine crawl—appeared higher up on the page. Long tails notwithstanding, most of us are not hunting for the obscure but look at the first few organic results that appear on the left (not the paid ones in the right column or at the top, which appear in a different color).

The second form of search engine marketing is **paid search,** which works as a kind of auction, with a marketer bidding on a list of search words/terms in order to have a site appear in the hierarchy of paid search sites. For instance, we would like Teleflora to come up first when someone types "flowers" in a search engine. However, so would every one of our competitors. So we bid for the honor.

In the doldrums of August, that is a rather inexpensive proposition. But in the days leading up to Mother's Day, it can cost thousands of dollars a day to win that **keyword.**

If we want to buy the key words "water from Fiji," there isn't much competition, so the expense is low. If, however, we want FIJI Water to come up first on the search for "bottled water," we have to bid against huge players like Pepsi and Coke. The narrower the definition of your keyword or phrases, the cheaper the buy; conversely, the more general the category, the more expensive.

At our company, we sometimes buy thousands of words for each brand. Here is a checklist of things to consider for your **keyword plan**:

Your product **category** (flowers for Mother's Day); your **product's name** (the Watering Can Bouquet); **attributes and accessories** (Flowers in a Gift); **manufacturer's** name (Teleflora); **advertiser's site functionally** (Florist Shop Locator); **lifestyle terms** (Holiday entertaining); **motivators** (Valentine's gift for my girlfriend); **corporate initiatives** (sustainability); **geographical terms** (Los Angeles Florists); and don't forget the all-important **typos** (misspelled words such as "Pomegranet" or "Fugi Water").

Getting to the top of the search engine requires a longterm investment of time and energy. It involves the efforts of your online and consumer marketing teams, designers, merchandisers, corporate communications and Web development people. Your search engine optimization strategy should be integral to your Web site development. It is the best return on investment you can get from Web advertising.

Community is the heart of the Web, and the advertisers that find a natural home there will prosper. What began as a virtual hangout for teens has become a place for all kinds of people and groups to meet: those who love Sharpeis (as though that were possible), retired NASA engineers, rugby fans, eco-moms.

> Community is the heart of the Web, and the advertisers that find a natural home there will prosper.

The Center for the Digital Future's 2007 study found that membership in online communities had more than doubled in just the past three years. Just as striking, more than half of online community members log on to their community daily, with 55 percent saying they feel as "strongly" about their online community as they do about their real-world community.

Facebook, MySpace, and other social networking sites are the metaphorical town squares of the twenty-first century. But they are expansive enough to include tens of millions of people in the discussion. Nearly one quarter of eighteen- to thirty-four-year-olds now keeps a personal blog.

We saw the impact of social networking profoundly in the 2008 presidential campaign. Barack Obama's youth-powered campaign acquired one million donors before the general election campaign even began. But in addition to using the Web to generate donations and spread viral campaign advertising via YouTube, as McCain also did aggressively, Obama's campaign used the Web to organize volunteers to an unprecedented degree. Despite the tens of millions spent on television by both campaigns, the Web was in some ways the more important technology, facilitating finance, communication, and organization—all at low cost.

We've nurtured a community of POM drinkers—Club POM—who enjoy having access to health studies and appreciate early notification of new products and announcements. Just as music fans enjoy talking about their favorite stars, members of Club Pom enjoy exchanging their favorite pomegranate recipes and personal health revelations, and just chatting about events in their area.

There's no reason to limit consumer participation to chat, however. Like other brands, we've also found it's exciting to put your fans to work—as your ad agency. With a grand prize of $3,000, a laptop, and a three-month supply of POM Tea—a sum that seemed awfully inexpensive even before we saw the high quality of work that contestants put in—we solicited video ads for POM Tea. Naturally, we had no idea what we would get. That's the whole idea—it's a free-for-all. Letting go is the nature of the interactive world. What we received was not just gratifying but astounding. As the ads began pouring in, posted on YouTube, I would wake in the morning, go online, and see what hilarious and imaginative new work had been posted in the past twenty-four hours—all for the love of POM Tea.

What could be better than engaging with consumers in a creative embrace of your brand? In the end, we received 148 submissions, with subject matter ranging from a backwoods survivalist hunting "free radicals" with his POM Tea to a hip-hop homage to POM Tea's thirst-quenching pleasures. On a dedicated site, visitors voted for their favorite POM Tea ad. The winner was a deeply felt romantic comedy of the POM Juice meets POM Tea genre produced by Griffin Hammond of Normal (no kidding), Illinois.

"Teleflora Presents America's Favorite Mom" also enlisted consumers, who produced video and written tributes to their mothers and posted them on the "America's

Favorite Mom" site. Nothing I've experienced in business compares to this creative collaboration. It's thrilling to see your consumers behaving like your partners rather than mere shoppers. And if you don't get inspired by their talent and enthusiasm, you're not paying attention.

Unfortunately, we're hardly alone in recognizing the Web's "creative" potential. The Web, of course, is essentially an open invitation to all manner of deception, ax grinding, and cheap shots.

After the popularity of POM inspired countless pomegranate juice imitators, we tried to enlist the government to battle the flimflammers and their false claims. We went to the FDA, presented conclusive evidence of fraud by companies slapping the "100% Pomegranate" label on junk juice mixtures of grape and apple and pear, and pleaded with the regulators to investigate them. Alas, the juice market is not a high priority for an overburdened, understaffed, and inadequately funded regulatory agency that is trying to protect us from potentially deadly drugs and other dangers. The government made it clear it was not going to police the junk juices, no matter how outrageous their claims. We were on our own.

In 2007, we decided to take a stand. We sued one of our competitors, Purely Juice, in federal court and laid out the case against their "100% Pomegranate" juice. It turned out to be a tough case to defend, owing to the fact that Purely Juice's definition of "100%" was actually "0%." We won that one. But there are plenty of other juice companies playing fast and loose out there.

As I said earlier, WWW stands for Wild, Wild West,

and if that means we have to don a badge and act like the sheriff, so be it. But we can't catch all the bad guys. Since 2003, roughly one thousand pomegranate products have been introduced to the marketplace. Not bad for a fruit hardly anyone had heard of six years ago. If imitation is the sincerest form of flattery, consider me flattered. At the beginning of 2008, we launched our pomegranatetruth.com site to give consumers a place to go for honest answers. Here's a sample of what we say:

> *Not every brand is as honest as POM Wonderful. Three independent labs tested ten other brands claiming to have 100% pomegranate juice and found that eight out of ten had added sugar, colorants and other low-grade fruit juices. So, other juices may be less expensive than ours, but you get what you pay for.*

Ideally, we wouldn't have to do this, but the marketplace has always had its dark corners, and just as the Web gives bad actors a terrific way to disseminate lies and misrepresentations, it also affords the opportunity to shine a light on their actions and expose them for the charlatans they really are. POM may be out in the forefront of using the Web to alert consumers to the frauds in our industry. But I think other honest companies in other industries will aggressively follow suit in the years ahead.

As it turns out, there are worse things on the Internet than fraud. In 2006, we came face-to-face with the Web's dark side. People for the Ethical Treatment of Animals

(PETA) began attacking POM for engaging in medical tests on animals. Using its Web site as a launchpad, they worked to organize a boycott of POM, including pressuring retailers not to stock it and consumers not to drink it. Their tactics were revolting. On their site, they featured an image of our POM heart logo being squeezed—with blood dripping down the bottle onto a dead rat. (Subtlety is not their thing.)

Not long ago, the standard approach in a case like this was to ignore the problem and hope it would fizzle out and, eventually, fade away. After all, boycotts were hard to organize and even harder to sustain. And why would anyone want to boycott POM? Our medical research had been conducted with the goal of improving human health. We were the good guys.

So initially we remained silent. Stewart (my own personal John Wayne) didn't want to "negotiate with terrorists." He chose the legal approach, fighting them in court. He felt if we just waited them out, PETA would get bored and move on to their next cause. That was a mistake. Apparently animal rights activists aren't easily bored.

The hundreds of thousands of people who visited their site couldn't understand why a juice company would be conducting tests using animals. What they didn't know was that we had invested millions in medical research to understand the efficacy of Wonderful pomegranates in treating a host of medical issues. Animal tests were necessary for the kind of rigorous, peer-reviewed science we were financing. Animal studies are generally a prerequisite for human studies and human studies are considered essential. (We didn't invent this protocol; but for the science to be considered sound, we had to follow it.) The news that we had done some animal tests struck many people as bizarre—as if we were engaged in gratuitous cruelty.

This was a fact that finally hit home with me when I was dining with News Corporation CEO Rupert Murdoch in the midst of the turmoil. Rupert is one of our most devoted customers. He keeps POM on his plane, in his office, and at his homes. He understands the medical advantages of drinking eight ounces a day. Rupert knew we were going through a hard time—he had read about it in Page 6 gossip in his own *New York Post*.

"Why do you have to do animal testing on your juice?" he asked. If someone as smart and committed to the juice as Rupert Murdoch was mystified, I realized, then plenty of other people were, too.

By retreating from the fight, we had ceded the field to our opponents. Misleading images and "facts" were soon disseminated over the Internet, including a video on the PETA Web site that implied that we had conducted research on dogs, cats, and primates. (Aside from one rabbit study exploring POM's positive effect on erectile dysfunction, all of the test subjects had been rats or mice.)

The PETA campaign was loaded with falsehoods, whether intentionally or simply as a result of the group's lackadaisical research. But what PETA's attack inspired was far worse. Animal rights extremists, some with their faces covered to avoid identification, began protesting outside our home. It was unnerving to drive each day past a group of screaming protesters who called us murderers and worse. Our grandchildren were scared to death whenever they visited. We felt like we were under house arrest.

Then the extremists descended on our employees. With bullhorns in their hands and bandannas over their cowardly faces, they confronted POM employees in their neighborhoods. The protesters were so proud of their intimidation raids that they videotaped them and uploaded the video—where else?—onto the Web. In one YouTube video, they can be seen hurling invective in front of modest homes in a modest neighborhood, against families with no protection.

They organized meetings through chat rooms and on MySpace and Craigslist. Our employees even endured death threats, some of them whispered through the windows of homes late at night. Meantime, at our headquarters, we received bomb threats. At one point, a group calling itself the Animal Rights Militia said it had poisoned five hundred bottles of POM in supermarkets on the East Coast. It turned out to be a terrible hoax.

Other strong-arm tactics were aimed at our retailers and consumers. Many of our retailers were determined not to give in to the threats. But as time went on and the protests continued, we could sense that some were beginning to cave. We tried every legal tool at our disposal, but nothing could stop the attacks. It was clear that the old ways simply didn't work in this new arena. Ironically, we had ceased animal testing on our juice six months before and had no plans to resume it in the future. So we adopted a two-part strategy to fight them in the same venue where we were being attacked—online.

We sent a detailed letter to our customers, which was also posted on our Web site, explaining everything—what research we had done and why—and refuting PETA's false claims. Then we posted a letter on our Web site and every relevant blog stating that we had stopped animal testing and had no plans to begin again.

The result? The Klan-like mob gatherings stopped. The boycott, which had lasted more than eight months, ended in three days.

But the experience revealed to me how much leverage a small, vocal, and relentless fringe can exert in the Internet Age. Mark Twain said, "One of the most striking differences between a cat and a lie is that a cat has only nine lives." On the Internet, you can drive a stake through the heart of a lie and watch it get up off the ground and race around the globe another time. I am unyielding in my support for the First Amendment. But the campaign of intimidation made me realize the price free speech can exact.

Despite the despicable tactics employed against us, I learned that even your worst enemies have something to teach you, if you listen carefully. We are more sensitive to the plight of lab animals now and more committed to doing all we can to protect their welfare. We contribute to a group seeking ways to advance the efficacy of test-tube science in the hope that, one day, medical tests on animals will no longer be necessary.

> Even your worst enemies have something to teach you,
> if you listen carefully.

The PETA campaign taught us other lessons, as well. Today we no longer wait for trouble to develop; we confront it head on. In 2007, at a panel discussion at the Aspen Ideas Festival, an annual event sponsored by the Aspen Institute, I heard the kernel of an attack with the potential to grow into a big problem. A young executive from Google was complaining about the environmental impact of bottled water. He cited an image he had recently created on a blog that showed a single bottle of our water three-fourths filled with crude oil. That, he claimed, was the amount of oil it took to bring our precious water from Fiji. He went on to urge that fresh water could be had—with no adverse effects—by simply turning on the tap. The moment was especially ironic because FIJI Water is a sponsor of the festival—our bottles were all over the dais. During his dissertation, the young critic was downing our water like a thirsty dog.

At the time, Al Gore's powerful film *An Inconvenient Truth* was igniting discussion of sustainability in living rooms and even boardrooms around the nation. The dialogue was long overdue—and it was expanding in all sorts of directions. For the first time, consumption patterns were coming under scrutiny.

Then Alice Waters, the famed owner of Chez Panisse in Berkeley, announced that she would no longer serve bottled water at her restaurant. It was one thing for a young guy on a panel to make noise. But Alice Waters is one of the most respected voices on food and sustainability in the world. If she said we had a problem, then we had a problem—and we had to deal with it.

As expected, the Chez Panisse news traveled all over the Internet, and what started as a trickle of criticism soon morphed into a gusher of dissent. With the credibility of Alice Waters behind it, the campaign was not limited to hard-core activists or extremists, as the PETA campaign had been. *Salon*, the online magazine, ran a column explaining how terrible bottled water is. The *New York Times* seemed to have an article about the issue every week. And my favorite newsman, Jim Lehrer, had a whole segment on his PBS show featuring San Francisco mayor Gavin Newsom holding his arms around a huge, imaginary ball, explaining the enormous amount of fuel required to transport a bottle of his "favorite" FIJI Water to his grocery store. As sometimes happens in the media, no one bothered to get the real facts or even to call us for our side of the story.

Fortunately, I had launched a hunt for the truth as soon as my alarm went off that day in Aspen. Our in-house consulting team was assigned to determine FIJI Water's actual carbon footprint. The claims being made about the amount of fuel required to ship it seemed impossible. For starters, if we were burning through that much oil, how could the business possibly survive, let alone make a profit?

Our team analyzed every detail in the production process and transportation of our water. They came up with a very different conclusion: our carbon footprint, including oil, accounted for just a tiny fraction of each bottle of FIJI Water. From the manufacture in China of preforms for our bottles until delivery of the finished product to the most distant retailer in the United States, a tablespoon of crude oil per bottle was consumed.

Because we use square bottles, we are able to pack them more tightly and ship them more efficiently. And because most of the miles we cover are nautical, rather than highway, we produce fewer emissions per ton carried and mile traveled. The container ships that transport our water from Fiji are seven times as environmentally efficient as trucks. Lately, we've been working to use rail transit on the mainland as much as possible. Trains are much better for the environment than trucks—and they reduce road congestion, too.

Armed with accurate data, we began to push back against the notion that bottled water presents an exaggerated threat to the environment. We used our FIJI Water Web site to make a comprehensive case for our FIJI Green initiative and lay out the facts about our energy policy and carbon footprint.

Because nothing ever dies on the Internet, however, you tend to have to fight the same battles over and over and over again, as new users pick up old data and arguments that were previously refuted or discredited. Keeping track of blogs and message boards helps keep you informed. We keep a close eye on Technorati, a free Web service that searches and organizes blogs as well as tagged social media (Facebook, Twitter, and others). Technorati tracks the links among these sources and indexes them according to relevance. That way we can check what the Web is saying about our brands.

It's important to keep your own Web site stocked with up-to-date information. We make sure our consumers have access to accurate information about the products they love. After all, they are the ultimate third-party endorsers and brand ambassadors. We make sure they can find the facts they need to argue our case.

But just as the fight against PETA alerted us to steps we could take to better protect animals, the controversy over bottled water got us thinking about how we could engineer our processes to do more for the environment—both in Fiji and elsewhere. In partnership with Conservation International, we accelerated our FIJI Green initiative.

It's not about spin. In order to be worthy of our consumers' affection, we had to go above and beyond expectations. By committing FIJI Water to a carbon-negative future, not decades from now but *today*, we took control of the issue and neutralized the attacks. We resolved to be defined by our actions—and our actions put us on the leading edge, the *greening* edge—of business ethics and corporate behavior in the world.

Now, in addition to stale complaints about bottled water, the Internet is buzzing with news and commentary about FIJI Water's leadership in tackling the environmental crisis of our time. In the raw and often crude marketplace of ideas that is the Internet, we're making our case—and we're winning.

For reasons I'll discuss in the following chapters, sustainability and business ethics are going to become more important, not less, in this new world. And partly because of the power of the Internet, the half-life of crooks and charlatans is going to shrink. In the old days, a huckster could take his medicine wagon from town to unsuspecting town, leaving a trail of victims in his wake. There is only one great big town now. If you're exposed once on the Internet, you're exposed for good.

On the other hand, if you're attacked unfairly, it's hard to remove the stain in cyberspace. There are plenty of reckless and irresponsible voices on the Web, as Andrew Keen documents in *The Cult of the Amateur: How Today's Internet Is Killing Our Culture*. But if the power of the Internet isn't always used responsibly, well . . . what power is?

CHAPTER 9

Green Is the New Black

General Electric and General Motors are two of the great industrial giants of the twentieth century. Unlike Microsoft, Google, and other Information Age behemoths, GE and GM run enormous factories where laborers churn out massive material goods—locomotives and turbines from GE, Hummers and Escalades from GM. Their products are forged steel, measured by the ton.

Now consider how these two aging titans have approached the twenty-first century. In 2002, when Enron was buried under the weight of its own fraud, GE purchased the company's wind energy business (yes, Enron apparently had a few assets other than greed) for nearly $400 million. Over the next several years, GE began investing heavily in alternative energy—photovoltaics, hydrogen fuel cells, and gasification equipment to increase the efficiency of coal-fired power plants and reduce their greenhouse gases.

In 2005, GE CEO Jeffrey Immelt launched the company's *ecomagination* initiative, promising to intensify the company's investment in green technologies while restraining GE's own greenhouse gas emissions. "We are launching ecomagination," Immelt said, "not because it is trendy or moral, but because it will accelerate our growth and make us more competitive."

Then there is GM. In recent years, the company has been eclipsed by more innovative competitors—Toyota and Honda in the first rank—selling cars that are better engineered, more reliable, and significantly more fuel-efficient. Even before the price of crude oil spiked, GM's gas-guzzling Hummer had become the symbol of wasteful, indulgent, and environmentally hazardous consumption.

The news of changing times somehow failed to get through to GM headquarters. In February 2008, the same month that the price of a barrel of oil burst through the $100 threshold, GM's vice chairman was quoted in the press calling global warming "a total crock of shit." What a charmer. This seems an apropos moment to mention that the company lost $38.7 *billion* in 2007.

Now, which of these companies founded in the era of heavy industry, GE or GM, do you suspect is more likely to navigate the challenges of the coming decades and live to see the start of another century? (You guessed right.)

Americans are very much aware of global warming and

other environmental challenges. But because public policy in the United States emanates from Washington, D.C., and since the White House and Congress have for years been almost criminally negligent in confronting these issues, we have not had the kind of public debate—let alone the sense of national mission—necessary to begin the transformation to a sustainable economy.

It wasn't long ago that Vice President Dick Cheney dismissed conservation as no more than "personal virtue" with absolutely no role to play in national energy policy. The comment was controversial at the time. But in retrospect, from the vantage point of a few more years of painfully high energy prices, increasingly shaky supplies, and the uninterrupted march of global warming, Mr. Cheney's remark appears not just cavalier but irredeemably stupid. It's the sort of thing that will find its way into history books a hundred years from now—provided we still have books and a civilization to read them—as evidence of ineptitude and ignorance at a pivotal moment in history.

While the Bush White House took its lackadaisical lead from the likes of General Motors, across the Atlantic, where energy use per capita is already half that in the United States, the future has been taking shape. In the United Kingdom, the public and private sectors have been busy constructing the institutional framework for managing a new environmental regime, including creation of the Carbon Trust, a government-funded company dedicated to helping industry and government lower carbon emissions.

Instead of wallowing in denial, Downing Street spent the past decade retooling to succeed in a difficult new environment. On a symbolic level alone, the differences are stark. British prime minister Gordon Brown has solar panels on his home in Scotland. Brown, of course, is the leader of the Labor Party, which you might expect to be more ardently green than the conservative opposition. But when it comes to leadership on the environment, Tory leader David Cameron is no Dick Cheney. The conservative leader has a wind turbine on the roof of *his* home and makes a point, when he can, of riding a bicycle to work.

Lest anyone miss the point, Cameron spelled it out in plain English. "There is no longer a rational case for business to fail to recognize the threat of climate change," he wrote. "Each company will have to play its part in reducing its own footprint; getting more value out of less resource; cutting energy and water usage; reducing packaging and waste; and becoming more efficient and profitable as a result."

In the absence of U.S. leadership on global warming and the environment, much of the world has moved forward regardless—including the business world. GE was hardly alone in recognizing the dawn of a new era.

In 2007, venture capitalists invested $2.2 billion in green technologies in the U.S. alone. Kleiner Perkins Caufield & Byers, the famed Silicon Valley venture investors, earmarked one third of the $1 billion the firm manages for green technology. Conferences on sustainability abound, where the corporate types talk about the environment and the environmentalists talk about sustainable business models. And it's no coincidence that the company that engineered and marketed the Prius automobile is among the most respected businesses and most valuable brands in the world.

States and localities have been stepping in to fill the void left by the federal government. California has adopted a broad range of measures to restrict greenhouse gases. New York City has pledged to reduce its carbon emissions by 30 percent by 2030. (According to *The New York Times*, because of the density of the city, New Yorkers already produce far less GHG than average—7.1 metric tons per person annually compared to 24.5 metric tons for the average American. Remember, they walk everywhere or take the subway.)

Even smaller cities and towns have joined the campaign. Nearly eight hundred towns have signed on to the U.S. Conference of Mayors' Climate Protection Agreement, which pledges to meet Kyoto standards for carbon emissions by 2012. Levittown, New York, that quintessential suburb of the 1950s, promised to stake its claim to the twenty-first century by reducing emissions by 10 percent in 2008.

Stewart and I recently attended a public lecture at Caltech where the professor said, "I don't know if the dire predictions of climate change will occur, but if there is a ten percent chance that they will, aren't we playing the most dangerous game of Russian roulette in the history of man?"

It's impossible to know precisely what the future holds. Maybe we'll get out of this mess—through the grace of nature or the technological ingenuity of humanity—without paying too dear a price. Then again, maybe we won't. In the face of potential disaster, common sense dictates a prudent course. Unfortunately, the prudent course right now is one of radical change. For any business, large or small, that means treating global warming like a deadly and imminent threat—and, of course, since we are in *business*, after all, also as a golden opportunity.

Regardless of whether or not the earth is on its way to being suffocated under a blanket of CO_2, the effects of global warming on the conduct of business will be enormous. In the past, no one really cared about the way we ran our businesses. Sure, if you cheated on your taxes or were one of those abusive executives exposed in the tabloids, you got some negative attention. But our operations were generally a private matter. And if our neighbors didn't care what we did, those on the other side of the planet cared even less.

Now my business and your business is *everybody's* business. If a factory in China is pumping gobs of CO_2 into the atmosphere and sending toxic effluents downstream to the fish farm that supplies my local supermarket, I have a vested interest in that factory's operations. In fact, a few billion people around the world might well conclude that they have a vested interest in that factory's operations. And they might decide it's in their collective interest for that factory to clean up its act or be shut down.

I must admit that "going green" to some extent has become a clever marketing ploy. But even when the motives are suspect, the change still helps us all in the end. A large water company recently took a fair amount of plastic out of its bottles. Now the bottles are so thin that if you grab them too firmly the water spouts out as soon as you open the top. But that's okay; if you don't mind a damp shirt, it works.

We are entering a new era in which stress on the planet, and on the humans and animals that inhabit it, is going to rise. Serious issues of production and consumption, energy use and waste, will be debated as never before. And the discussion will take place in front of a global audience of six billion people—perhaps rising to nine billion by midcentury—of which every single member has a profound personal stake in the outcome.

"Possessing an excessive carbon footprint is rapidly becoming the modern equivalent of wearing a scarlet letter," wrote Michael Specter in *The New Yorker.*

Business in the era of global warming will increasingly become public domain. When emissions from a factory in Topeka influence childhood asthma in Atlanta, crop yields in Uganda, and sea levels in Bangladesh, the notion that we're all connected has ceased to be a metaphor. If you can't justify your business operations and actions in that environment, you will pay a price in the developed world and, before long, in the developing world, as well. Because in the midst of a global environmental crisis, neither old world nor new, first or third, developed or developing, will tolerate rogue businesses sucking the very life out of the earth.

To put this in consumerist terms, if you're failing to deliver sufficient value to justify the toll you take on the environment, if you're squandering valuable communal resources to no great end, who on earth is going to buy what you have to sell? And how can you justify your company's existence?

It's in the myopic nature of humans to think that the way things are is the way they will be forever. But history tells us that that is never, ever the case. Change is constant. With that in mind, consider the fact that our mass consumer society is little more than a hundred years old. Our current way of life is nothing but "a time-bound historical creation," as William Leach wrote in *Land of Desire: Merchants, Power, and the Rise of a New American Culture.*

Consumer culture began in another era, when global issues of growth, energy consumption, and the environment were viewed in a completely different light and the ideal of "democratic abundance" was a distant goal. In a world constrained by global warming and other borderless environmental threats, consumption itself will be the subject of new and vigorous scrutiny. It has already been put under the microscope by best-selling authors Michael Pollan, Eric Schlosser, and Bill McKibben. A new generation is poised to enter the discussion, weighing the ethical and environmental consequences of our way of life.

As we grapple with these complex issues, brands will come under increasing pressure to deliver authentic, sustainable value. Environmental impact will increasingly become a basis for evaluating the goods and services we buy. And that scrutiny will begin with the final consumer product and work its way back down the supply chain—all the way to the raw materials that feed the manufacturing source. Companies will have to be able to justify their actions at each step of that process. And they will have to provide a measure of their environmental impact from start to finish.

> Environmental impact will increasingly become a basis for evaluating the goods and services we buy.

Tesco, the largest grocery chain in the United Kingdom, offers a glimpse of the very near future. The company has vowed to cut its own energy use in half by 2010. But that's just the start. In addition, Tesco has begun an expensive and labor-intensive effort to measure the carbon footprint of each of the seventy thousand products the chain stocks. It has also pledged to cut back on products that are shipped by air—the most GHG-intensive form of transportation.

For years, supermarkets like Tesco had an incentive to stock as many products as they could profitably sell. In the new era, that logic is beginning to erode—not only because products shipped by air will have to pass a new threshold to merit inclusion but because each and every product in the store will be measured by a new standard.

That standard is simply this: Is the product valuable

enough to justify its carbon footprint? What about new products? Is a new product, which must be introduced to consumers and must compete with established products, worth the shipping and shelf space it will require? Does it justify the creation of yet more carbon? Conversely, will old consumer standbys be displaced by new competitors bragging about their smaller carbon footprints?

These are new kinds of questions, and they will play a new role in shaping a new kind of economy. Many products—and companies—may find they do not have the right answers. Perhaps their production processes are too dirty, or their product is ultimately too inessential, to pass the carbon test. After all, Wal-Mart and Costco, two stores synonymous with "plenty," already restrict many category offerings to just two brands. Is it so hard to imagine supermarkets across the country following suit?

In the fall of 2005, Wal-Mart unveiled its own environmental plan. The world's largest retailer, said CEO Lee Scott, wants to be a "good steward for the environment," ultimately using only renewable energy sources and producing zero waste. The company teaches vendors how to go green and insists they follow Wal-Mart standards in order to be included in the inventory mix. (We know—we sell our products to them.) Of course, naysayers contend that Wal-Mart's initiative is a ploy to save money. Hey, wake up—going green does save money, and what's wrong with that?

To survive what may well be a brutal era of creative destruction—one that appears to be right around the corner—smart companies are already positioning themselves on the green side. We are doing everything we can to be one of them. Since I joined the board of Conservation International twelve years ago, I've been working to educate myself about environmental issues. Getting to know Sylvia Earle, the world's greatest oceanographer, whom I lovingly call "Her Deepness," has enlightened me to the sad plight of our oceans and the depletion of fisheries. Jared Diamond, another friend, has influenced me, as well. His landmark book *Collapse* is a jarring reminder of how previous civilizations were agents of their own demise. These are voices of our age—speaking out for all of us to hear and heed.

When we launched FIJI Green, we didn't really know what we were getting into. There was no one in the industry we could use as a model. (Coke? Pepsi? Pleeeease!) There was no Carbon Trust to provide advice or facilitate the process. There was no road map showing how to proceed. There weren't even any reliable data to indicate how expensive the transition would be.

We have the luxury of being a private company. We don't answer to the nearsighted pack on Wolf Street. So we decided to take the green plunge and deal with the consequences—come what may. Want to know how naive we were? Setting aside our conservation projects, including preservation of the Sovi Basin in Fiji, it turns out that FIJI Green's impact on our bottom line will be millions of dollars. Fortunately, the initiative will be *adding* millions to the bottom line, not *subtracting* them. As it turns out, we should have gone green long ago.

One of the most significant costs we have at FIJI is PET, the plastic resin that is an essential element of every bottle. PET is also a significant source of carbon. So by reducing the amount of PET in our bottles, we're going to reduce carbon and save money.

Similarly, our energy costs in Fiji are about twice as high as energy costs in California. By replacing our old energy infrastructure with wind turbines, we're going to save a lot of money on power over the long run—while simultaneously reducing carbon. I mentioned before that shipping by boat produces dramatically less carbon than shipping by truck. We're now serving not only the West Coast but the eastern seaboard, via the Panama Canal, by boat. By reducing our reliance on trucking, again, we're also reducing costs.

Lately, however, some environmentalists have taken issue with bottled water, citing two concerns. The first is that, unlike tap water, bottled water is, well, *bottled.* That means you create packaging to contain it and you dispose of that packaging after it's been consumed. Second is that, unlike tap water, bottled water must be transported from the source to the marketplace, thereby consuming energy and dispensing carbon into the atmosphere. I confess to being mystified by this argument. Here's why:

- People need to hydrate.
- In a mobile, fast-paced society, they frequently need to hydrate on the go, rather than in their kitchens.
- Even for those at home, tap water is suspect in many, many communities and a known hazard in others.

• Even when tap water is safe, it simply doesn't taste good to many people. They don't want to drink it.

In reality, bottled water does not even compete with the tap; it merely replaces less healthy beverages that are worse for the environment. According to Beverage Marketing Corporation, annual bottled water volume grew by 1.3 billion gallons over the past two years in the United States. Where did this volume come from? People aren't any thirstier, so the answer lies in the decline of other packaged beverages.

Carbonated soft drinks have lost 600 million gallons of consumption during the same period, and the full-calorie versions of these products have fared particularly badly. Sugary fruit beverages have lost an additional 200 million gallons. Meantime, there has been no material change in the consumption of tap water. In effect, the 1.3 billion additional gallons of water that consumers drank eliminated nearly one trillion calories from the American diet. But not only calories were eliminated.

The high-fructose beverage that water supplanted was likely soda, itself a packaged good that is transported to the marketplace. And harvesting, shipping, and transforming corn into syrup is an energy-intensive process.

What, then, would we achieve by removing bottled water from the marketplace, other than to encourage greater carbon and waste production accompanied by a rise in obesity, diabetes, and other health problems? Already, two liters of carbonated soft drink are sold for every liter of water. Is it really in society's interest to increase that ratio?

Bottled water accounts for two hundredths of 1 percent of U.S. oil consumption, and plastic water bottles make up one third of 1 percent of municipal waste streams. Even so, we're determined to do all we can to reduce FIJI's environmental impact.

· In addition to the previously mentioned measures, we're reducing the amount of overall packaging by 20 percent, and more of what remains will come from recycled materials. We already use rectangular bottles, which take up less space than round bottles and enable us to ship more product per cubic foot. We're also stepping up our efforts to encourage expanded curbside recycling and consumer incentive programs, such as container deposit laws that include water bottles.

Only eleven states have container deposit laws, and just four of those include water bottles. Yet most of the industry is opposed to recycling, since a container deposit raises the retail price of water bottles. We hope they'll see the light. Our laws, which preceded the emergence of the bottled-water industry, are antiquated. They need to be updated to account for the urgent environmental crisis we face.

The national recycling rate for plastic bottles is an abysmal 31 percent. Yet we know from Fiji's carbon footprint analysis that recycling a water bottle reduces its carbon footprint by at least one third. A ton of recycled plastic saves about 685 gallons of oil.

We're a small company. We represent only about 1 percent of the entire bottled water industry. Bottled water is here to stay; the industry is not going to disappear. On the contrary, it's going to continue growing as consumers become more aware of the health problems associated with soda and other artificially sweetened beverages. As consumers increasingly seek healthy alternatives, water will become a beverage of choice.

The transition to green isn't 100 percent perfect. We have to maintain higher inventories because our water, traveling by ship and, increasingly, by train, takes longer to reach its destination than it did when it traveled by truck. But that's a very small price to pay to be both carbon-negative and, in the long run, more profitable.

Our large customers have been very supportive, in part because they are getting pressure from *their* customers to show they are responding to the environmental challenge. Restaurant and hotel patrons are aggressively seeking green alternatives to the status quo. And, believe me, we all need them. Today, if you are served a liter of FIJI Water in a restaurant, that product represents carbon emissions of *negative* 114 grams as a result of our FIJI Green initiative. But what about that eight-ounce, grain-fed steak on your plate? That's a different story. By the time it's served up medium rare, your steak has left a trail of 8,300 grams of carbon in its wake. You would have to drink twenty-seven half-liter bottles of water to achieve the same environmental impact.

FIJI Water has begun offering advice to customers who want to reduce their own carbon footprint. In March 2008, we became the first privately held company to join the Carbon Disclosure Project, a voluntary organization dedicated to reducing carbon in business and encouraging carbon transparency. But we could sure use more support from other businesses and from the government. The best way, for example, to reduce carbon emissions in the bottled beverage industry is to use plastic instead of glass bottles and then to recycle them.

Until Google surpassed us with its own solar field last year, we were the proud owners of the largest solar field in California. Covering seven acres, the field provides 30 percent of the power to process our pistachio crop. We are currently building a new juicing plant for POM Wonderful that will burn discarded pistachio shells as part of our alternative power mix. We have transitioned POM Tea from glass containers to plastic. Our in-house consulting group has a division that focuses on sustainability. Its mission is to evaluate the carbon footprint of all our businesses, illustrate how sustainability can benefit our brands, strengthen our relationships with customers and consumers, cut costs, and realize our commitment to being a responsible company.

In addition, in California's Central Valley, we have built a totally green preschool for the children of our employees. Our corporate headquarters building is going green floor by floor. We're trying to do better at home, too. Almost every car in our family is a hybrid. Stewart and I are constantly reducing our energy use at home by changing appliances (the average refrigerator accounts for 15 percent of home energy consumption), redoing our windows with double panes, using energy-efficient lightbulbs, and so on.

Now that the head-in-the-sand era of Bush and Cheney is over, government will be able to do more to spur innovation and initiate changes to begin reining in greenhouse gases. But the private sector can't afford to wait. With the federal government no longer an obstacle, change is coming quickly. We're all going green—like it or not.

And if you don't believe in global warming? Well, you don't have to. Global warming is not the only factor influencing the green imperative. A number of geologists believe we have hit a point of "peak oil," meaning that our ability to extract the black gold that fueled industry and growth in the twentieth century is about to decline. Established oil fields are producing less, and new fields are increasingly rare. Production from oil sands and other alternative, difficult-to-extract sources is inefficient and expensive. Biofuels, depending upon the source, are costly and energy-intensive themselves (and can contribute to global warming instead of mitigating it).

Meanwhile, global demand for energy has soared in recent years. Oil consumption in high-growth economies, including China and India, has risen at roughly six times the rate of growth in developed economies. China already consumes more grain, coal, and steel than the United States and is putting huge numbers of new cars on its congested roads. Tata, India's largest industrial conglomerate, recently introduced a $2,500 automobile that promises to increase that nation's already enormous appetite for oil. As a consequence, even without global warming, we seem to be hurtling toward a serious global energy crisis that will change the shape of economies in the future.

Like the remorseless logic of global warming, the logic of energy shortage steers us back to consumption. Tens of thousands of new products are introduced each year. Given the energy required to produce them and the waste entailed in packaging and shipping, how many of these products will consumers decide they really need? How many are truly valuable and necessary in an economy defined by scarce energy supplies and environmental crisis?

> Even if you don't believe that we are in the early stages of environmental crisis, it makes sound strategic sense to behave as if we are. So go ahead. Fake it.

"In many respects, the scientific debate is irrelevant," wrote Andrew J. Hoffman of the University of Michigan, author of a chapter entitled "The Coming Market Shift: Business Strategy and Climate Change" in *Cut Carbon, Grow Profits: Business Strategies for Managing Climate Change and Sustainability.* "The debate is thus strategic (not scientific) and companies taking voluntary climate action are not practicing philanthropy or pure social responsibility (although many couch their activities in the language of 'doing the right thing'). In fact, many companies are agnostic about the science of climate change. They engage the climate change issue as a way to protect their strategic investments and to search for business opportunities in a changing market landscape."

In other words, even if you don't believe, as I do, that we are in the early stages of environmental crisis, it makes sound strategic sense to behave as if we are. Go ahead, fake it.

Keep in mind that the definition of value has already begun to expand. In the future, it will no longer be restricted to the product or service you provide. It will include the toll taken on energy supplies and the global environment in the process. In this new era, climate science will exert enormous influence over companies, markets and even international trade. Bestselling author and *New York Times* columnist Thomas Friedman has said that green is the new red, white, and blue. But for business, green is the new black.

CHAPTER 10

Nurturing Brand Faith in an Age of Cynicism

There is a long list of American leaders in politics, business, sports, and the arts who have contributed more than their share to the erosion of public trust. Bill Clinton lied. George W. Bush lied. Ken Lay lied. Bernie Ebbers lied. Dennis Kozlowski lied. Many people assume that Barry Bonds and Roger Clemens lied. And it seems as if the audience of readers for anguished personal memoirs is supplied by an ever-expanding army of authors, some of whom, like James Frey, are willing to fabricate a few of the million little pieces of narrative that constitute a "nonfiction" book.

We've always been a nation of tall tales and confidence men—Paul Bunyan and P. T. Barnum, Johnny Appleseed and Donald Trump. Everyone loves a good yarn. When canned tuna was introduced to the marketplace, it battled for share with the reigning king of canned fish, salmon.

Tuna wrested the crown away by proclaiming that it was "guaranteed not to turn pink in the can." That story, by the way, is every bit as fishy as its subject. Yet it's been told countless times with endless variations and grace notes simply because we marketers enjoy telling it so much.

Each generation seems convinced that the world it has inherited is speeding to Hell in the latest handbasket, whether the vehicle is a chariot or a Hummer. Yet even with that in mind, the perception this time seems especially acute. In a 2007 Roper survey, 51 percent of Americans said they believed business ethics had gotten worse in the past five years. That's a pretty remarkable vote of no confidence in the business world, and the time frame—a mere five years!—is certainly impressive. Enron lives on.

In *Deep Economy*, Bill McKibben cites a lengthier and more ominous trend. The National Opinion Research Council has shown a steady decrease in happiness among Americans since the 1950s. The decline was accompanied by a doubling of median income in the same period, which may be the best proof yet that money can't buy you love or happiness.

Disillusionment with a half century of American politics and government surely plays a part. But business has provided ample kindling for cynicism. Grotesquely overpaid CEOs, unethical behavior, and lousy, even dangerous, products bear much of the blame. So does marketing.

Nearly a third of American adults are obese, according to the Centers for Disease Control and Prevention. Yet Pepsi and Coca-Cola spend billions of dollars a year marketing junk food and endless varieties of high-fructose corn syrup to people who are literally dying from the pleasure.

The lists of ingredients in "100% Natural" 7 UP, "healthy and delicious" Egg Beaters, "wholesome" granola bars, and vitamin "fortified" chocolate milk are sufficient to fell a mature water buffalo.

Brands that were once synonymous with American culture and optimism have undermined their own value and cast a pall over consumer products generally. The road to ill health is paved with Doritos. In the film *Super Size Me*, the filmmaker ends up in the hospital as a result of a steady diet of what passes for food at McDonald's. Ford and GM, once icons of glamour and quality around the world, have become symbols of self-doubt and, in their refusal to take responsibility for the automobile's impact on the planet, of self-delusion and environmental destruction.

Perhaps no industry exemplifies the damage done by marketing and manipulation more than pharmaceuticals. Americans are living longer lives today, and managing chronic diseases better, in very large part due to the genius of drug company scientists and technologists in creating new products to treat everything from high blood pressure to cancer. Yet despite having extended and improved the lives of tens of millions of people, the industry is reviled for its predatory marketing practices and held in contempt for its obstruction of any sincere effort to resolve the problem of 47 million uninsured Americans. It's not easy to elicit disgust from someone whose life you have just saved.

Between corrupting the medical profession, stalling the introduction of generic drugs, and spending millions on dubious, direct-to-consumer advertising, drug companies have somehow managed to pull it off.

My point? Marketing overstepped its natural boundaries. Drug companies have transformed patients into brand-conscious consumers, looking for the equivalent of a Gucci logo at their local pharmacy. Disney and MTV have transformed childhood into a marketplace of branded experiences. And brands have worked their way into the emotionally charged space in our lives that was once reserved for family, friends, and community. You think you've been welcomed into the warm embrace of the Pepsi Generation, but instead all you get is more calories than your body can burn. By encouraging consumers to build emotional relationships with brands, marketers have set us—and themselves—up for a fall. Too often, brands promise more than they can ever hope to deliver.

"Branding works its magic only up to the point of sale," McKibben wrote, "and then actual human need returns, unfulfilled; the advertiser is always pleased to offer a new round of promise and failure, but after a century it's probably time to pursue some other strategy."

There are only two explanations for a breakdown in the relationship between a brand and a consumer: Either the consumer has run out of money, or she has run out of faith. Betrayal is an unpleasant experience—whether the betrayer is a spouse, a friend, or a familiar brand. Yet the way the world is changing raises the stakes for brands that don't deliver real value. There will always be snake oil salesmen—and some portion of them will get away with their game for a while. But on an increasingly transparent globe, where information is available every-where, that becomes significantly harder to do.

> Betrayal is an unpleasant experience—whether the betrayer is a spouse, a friend, or a familiar brand.

A disgruntled former employee armed with unflattering data and a blog can do millions of dollars in damage with a few words. As everyone knows, once information appears on the Internet, it's a permanent record. If you're not hon-oring your word, sooner or later the world will find you out.

Consumer power will continue to grow as a result of this new technology. The consumer protection move-ment, which started long before Ralph Nader, has ebbed and flowed with business cycles and cultural tides. It is due for resurgence. Under the threat of global warming and the reality of growing inequality, consumers have ev-ery reason to be interested in more than a bargain base-ment price. Prior to World War II, *Consumer Reports* rated products not only on the quality of their performance but also on the quality of their manufacturers' labor relations. After decades of declining labor power, pension rip-offs, and the erosion of middle- and working-class wages and job security, a similarly holistic approach to product evaluation is in store.

With the Internet clearing the way to greater transparency, the public will be privy to a broad range of quality assessments of a brand. Whether a brand delivers on its value promise will be chief among them. But in addition, many consumers will also want to know the measure of a brand's carbon footprint and how a company deals with its workers and local communities. Similarly, in order for companies to take advantage of the community brain power models of Wikinomics and so-called naked transparency, in which outside collaborators contribute to business projects managed on the Web like an open book, they will need to be models of ethics and social responsibility.

Brands that set high standards for themselves are doing well these days. Patagonia's promise of clothes manufactured in an ethical and environmentally sound manner, including the use of recycled materials, seems right in sync with the times. Target appears similarly intent on pairing value and values for less affluent consumers. Entrepreneurs are merging business and philanthrophy into new, hybrid models. For every pair of TOMS Shoes you purchase, the company donates a pair to a needy child in South America or Africa.

It's not always easy to do the right thing in business. Believe me, I know. One episode from my own experience that gives me a queasy feeling in my stomach to this day occurred at the Frankin Mint many years ago. We had been doing a great business in collector plates—so good, in fact, that we launched a program of "forced conversion," similar to that used by book clubs, record clubs, and the like.

By ordering one plate in a twelve-plate series, a collector automatically received the next eleven. This plan was flawed from the start. First, there was no way for our artist to create the art for twelve plates in such a limited time. The plates were fine art fired into porcelain—not cookie-cutter representations. Second, who wants to order one plate and a week later find, unsolicited, a box of eleven others on the doorstep? It was a terrible idea. I should have stopped it before it ever started.

In the end, we got our just desserts. Collectors were understandably annoyed, and the business suffered as a result. In fact, I can pinpoint that lapse in judgment as the moment when our lucrative collector plate business started going down the tubes.

Transparency is a lot easier to talk about than it is to realize. It can be awkward for all the obvious reasons—and even some not so obvious ones. I have always believed that if you get your accolades on Earth, by the time you get to Heaven the folks up there may not be thrilled to see you. Stewart and I have generally preferred anonymity when making charitable donations. That seems like a luxury we can no longer afford.

In an era in which attacks can come seemingly from nowhere, speed throughout the Internet, and hobble your business in days, you need to be able to draw on a reservoir of goodwill. To draw on it, however, you will first have to establish it through very public conduct.

We plan to be more forthcoming about our own activities. In addition to our gifts to large institutions, such as the Los Angeles County Art Museum and UCLA's medical center, we do a lot with our employees, including encouraging their own philanthropy. In our Roll Giving program, every employee receives $1,000 per year to give to the charity of his or her choice (provided it's not political or religious). Additionally, we match employees' personal charitable donations up to $5,000 per year.

In the California Central Valley, any employee's child who maintains a 2.8 grade point average receives a college scholarship. Once enrolled in college, we provide counseling to the students, many of whom are the first in their families to pursue higher education. We want to help them succeed. In addition, we have helped put arts back into the public schools through our association with P.S. Arts, created an after-school reading program, built a preschool, and created a program with Bard College to train seventy-five teachers a year who will work in schools in the Valley. We recently provided the funds for a 50,000-square-foot wing for the Children's Hospital in Madera, California. We focus much of our philanthropy on the Central Valley because we are the largest employer there. We also know that many who live in the Valley are ignored by government.

Perhaps it's ironic that a technological revolution is ushering in the values of a forgotten, preindustrial era. By reducing the amount of communicating we do face-to-face, the Internet has encouraged vicious gossip, baseless attacks, and unhinged polemics from every corner. But by making the world smaller, it is also reinforcing a certain level of small-town business mores. Who runs an honest shop and who is a cheat? Who looks out for the less fortunate and who is a Scrooge? In a small town, everyone knows the answers. So it will be in the Internet Age. Brands that fail to establish good faith will confront a public that is well informed, skeptical, and unforgiving.

> By making the world smaller, the Internet is also reinforcing a certain level of small-town business mores.

Ethical and socially responsible behavior will enable you to function and communicate in this environment. But it won't necessarily ensure that you will profit in it. In 2006, 182,000 new consumer packaged goods products were introduced in stores around the world, a new record. How long a tail will a stressed planet support? Value is the ultimate bedrock. Value builds faith, and faith builds the kind of solid, long-term equity that can withstand competition and overcome challenges.

When all is said and done, there is only one sure route to survival in any market, and one hedge against irrelevance and obsolescence: cultivate the rubies in the orchard. Locate the intrinsic value of your brand, work to understand it and nurture it—even when that brand is you yourself. Communicate that value honestly and creatively. If you do, you will build the kind of faith in your brand that can overcome tough competition, hard times, cheap shots, and even a roller coaster of a new century.

ACKNOWLEDGMENTS

Unless you are painting the *Mona Lisa*, there is no creative process you complete alone. Even then, someone has to stretch your canvas and clean your brushes—and there is always the crucial matter of inspiration.

I have been blessed with help from many people, starting with my parents. My father taught me not to be afraid of anyone or anything. I also inherited his creative genes and artistic talent. My mother has a legendary sense of humor, and is no slouch in the creative department, either. She never met a house she couldn't redecorate. I have been inspired throughout my life by her sense of style and design.

When Stewart and I married thirty-five years ago, we joined our families—and from the outset it just worked. My sons, Jason and Jonathan, were thrilled to have siblings so close in age, and Jeff, Ilene, and Bill immediately warmed to me and my boys. We have been a closely knit mélange ever since. Our children have gracefully accepted the mother who works, and our lives together have been more than I ever dreamed possible. I love my children with all my heart. I couldn't be more proud of the amazing adults they have become, and their wonderful mates—Blue, Daniel, Chris, and Doug—are great additions to our family circle.

My grandchildren are a constant inspiration. I hope that today, at seventeen, with her creativity spilling over into every activity of her life, Danielle no longer bemoans the fact that I am "not like normal grandmas, baking cookies and sitting on the porch knitting" till she comes home from school. Scarlett, on the other hand, told me the other day, "I don't want to be like you . . . I want to be you!" Now, that is a compliment. Lucy and Oliver are a constant source of joy and amazement.

I want to thank my team at Roll for making so many successes possible: Bryan Honkawa, my muse and head designer; David Layton, whose work on the book jacket and color insert was inspired; Liz Leow and Mike Perdigao, whose brilliant efforts in advertising, Web development, and photography were so essential. So many talented individuals in our in-house agency—aptly called FIRE STATION—have helped. There is no team on or off Madison Avenue that does it better.

Tom Mooney was the life force behind our green transformation at FIJI. Without his steadfast commitment, it would have taken many more months or years to complete our goal. Matt Tupper has been my partner at POM since 2003. His sense of honor and faith in the brand have enabled us to move light-years ahead. I thank Brian Fisher, Peter Sauerborn, and Lilie Rahimzadeh for their immeasurable help in creating the Internet primer. David Pinion is my proofreader par excellence. Craig Cooper is more than in-house counsel; he is *consigliere* to the Roll family of companies. Shawn Weidmann, Teleflora's president, and John Cochran, president of FIJI Water, offered support and tolerated their staffs' time-consuming contributions to this effort.

Without Rob Six, I wonder how I could have done all the work that comes after a book is done. He is a brilliant public-relations guru, a dear friend, and a tireless supporter. Julie Fields and Fiona Posell helped before and after the writing was done as well. Anita Ferry, my personal assistant, has been tireless in her work behind the scenes. She is simply the best.

Our family doctor, Leslie Dornfeld, who passed away a few years ago, was really the catalyst in discovering the health properties of the pomegranate. He and his lovely wife, Maria Grazie, are remembered and missed every day of my life. Dr. Harley Liker, together with Mark Dreher, shares my enthusiasm for the pomegranate's virtues and has directed the astounding scientific research on pomegranates and human health.

So many of my dear friends have believed in this project and shown their love and support. Thanks to Wendy Goldberg, Shelli Azoff, Lyn Lear, Jane Nathanson, Irena

Medavoy, Arianna Huffington, Lori Milken (a great, if undiscovered, writer), Marlene Malek, and Jan Greenberg (who reads all I write and offers sound advice based on her great writing talent). These are my dearest buddies. I never had time for girlfriends until my children were safely out of the house. I missed a lot by not seeking them out sooner, but what a great bonanza it is to have their love in my life.

I am also inspired by some men in my life: Leonard Goldberg, who read my first drafts and was clear and fair in his advice; Mike Milken, who proves that one person can really make a difference in this world; Norman Lear, whose extraordinary grace defies age; and Walter Isaacson, who has inspired me through his actions and shown me the need for every individual to care as deeply about the common good as they care about their own family.

People ask, "How long did it take you to write this book?" I answer, "All my life." The actual collaboration with Frank Wilkinson was an amazing, seamless process because Frank is such a pro, an exceptional writer—and so staggeringly smart. It also helped that I had written sixty pages before we met and had about six boxes overflowing with research ready when we began. Ivan Roth worked with me on those first drafts, and his humor and talent have been a huge delight.

Jennifer Walsh and Mel Berger, my agents at William Morris, whom I met through my dear friend Jim Wiatt, represented me beautifully and gave me great counsel about packaging the book. They also set up meetings with publishers. From the moment I met Roger Scholl, my editor at Doubleday, I knew he was the one. Roger has been there for me every step of the way, and I don't care who knows it—I worship him. There is a great team at Random House that also contributed to the success of this book.

The reason *Rubies in the Orchard* is dedicated to Stewart Resnick is because, above all others, he is my greatest friend, most honest critic, and the love of my life. Together we have created a wonderful family and a marriage and love affair worthy of great opera. In my career, he has been the rock of stability. I could never have done it without him. I certainly never wanted to.

ILLUSTRATION CREDITS

INDEX